MICHIGAN

D0940189

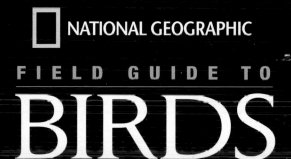

◻ NATIONAL GEOGRAPHIC

FIELD GUIDE TO

BIRDS

MICHIGAN

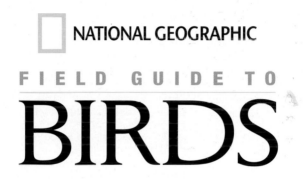

NATIONAL GEOGRAPHIC

FIELD GUIDE TO

BIRDS

Edited by JONATHAN ALDERFER

National Geographic
Washington, D.C.

Introduction

Michigan is well-known as the only breeding ground of the Kirtland's Warbler, but the state has much more to offer birders. Many warbler species breed in the transitional and coniferous forests of the north, while southern warblers breed in deciduous and riparian areas in the southernmost parts of the state. Most sought after among the 30 breeding species are Connecticut and Golden-winged Warblers in the north, and Cerulean, Yellow-throated, and Prothonotary Warblers in the south.

Scattered among the mixed and coniferous forests of the Upper Peninsula are patches of true boreal forest with their attendant species, including Spruce Grouse, Black-backed Woodpecker, Yellow-bellied Flycatcher, Boreal Chickadee, and Gray Jay. Every 3-5 years, northern owls move south in response to food shortages farther north. At such times, Snowy, Great Gray, Northern Hawk, and Boreal Owls can be found, mainly in the Upper Peninsula. Likewise, the so-called "winter finches," including Pine Grosbeak, Common Redpoll, Pine Siskin, Evening Grosbeak, and crossbills, move southward in similar "irruptions."

The most dominant features of Michigan's landscape are the Great Lakes themselves. Tremendous numbers of waterfowl use the lakes during migration, and good numbers of the less common sea ducks can also be found. With loons, grebes, scoters, and jaegers counted in significant numbers, the experience is akin to an Atlantic coast seawatch. The shoreline of Lake Erie provides a landfall for thousands of hawks migrating from Canada in one of the greatest migration spectacles in North America.

A total of 421 species have been documented in the Great Lakes State, plenty to hold the interest of birders.

Allen T. Chartier
Project Director
Great Lakes HummerNet

CONTENTS

LOOKING AT BIRDS

What do the artist and the nature lover share? A passion for being attuned to the world and all of its complexity, via the senses. Every time you go out into the natural world, or even view it through a window, you have another opportunity to see what is there. And the more you know what you are looking at, the more you see.

Even if you are not yet a committed birder, it makes sense to take a field guide with you when you go out for a walk or a hike. Looking for and identifying birds will sharpen and heighten your perceptions, and intensify your experience. And you'll find that you notice everything else more acutely—the terrain, the season, the weather, the plant life, other animal life.

Birds are beautiful, complex animals that live everywhere around us in our towns and cities, and in distant places we dream of visiting. Here in North America more than 900 species have been recorded—from abundant commoners to the rare and exotic. A comprehensive field reference like the *National Geographic Field Guide to the Birds of North America* is essential for understanding that big picture. If you are taking a spring walk in the Michigan countryside, however, you may want something simpler: a guide to the birds you are most likely to see, which slips easily into a pocket.

This photographic guide is designed to provide an introduction to the common birds—and a few rare birds—you might encounter in Michigan: how to identify them, how they behave, and where to find them, including specific locations.

Discovery, observation, and identification of birds can be exciting, whether you are a novice or expert. As an artist and birder for most of my life, I know that every time I go out to look at birds, I see more clearly and have a greater appreciation for the natural world around me and my own place in it.

JONATHAN ALDERFER
Editor

National Geographic's Field Guide to Birds: Michigan is designed to help birders at any level quickly identify birds in the field. The book is organized by bird families, following the order in the *Check-list to the Birds of North America,* by the American Ornithologists' Union. Families share structural characteristics, and by learning these shared characteristics early, birders will establish a basis for a lifetime of identifying birds and related family members with great accuracy—sometimes merely at a glance. (For quick reference in the field, use the color and alphabetical indexes at the back of this book.)

A family may have one member or dozens of members, or species. In this book each family is identified by its common name in English along the right-hand border of each spread. Each species is also identified in English, with its Latin genus and species—its scientific name—found directly underneath. One species is featured in each entry. An entry begins with

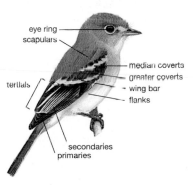

eye ring
scapulars

median coverts
greater coverts
wing bar
flanks

tertials

secondaries
primaries

Least Flycatcher

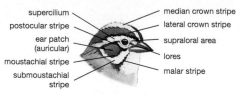

Lark Sparrow

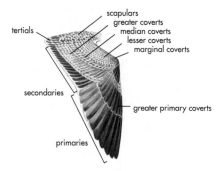

Great Black-backed Gull, upper wing

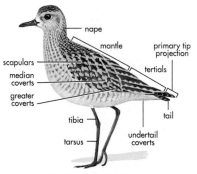

Pacific Golden-Plover

Field Marks, the physical clues used to quickly identify a bird, such as body shape and size, bill length, and plumage color or pattern. A bird's body parts yield vital clues to identification, so a birder needs to become familiar with them early on. After the first glance at body type, take note of the head shape and markings, such as stripes, eye rings, and crown markings. Bill shape and color are important as well. Note body and wing details: wing bars, color of primary flight feathers, wing color at rest, and shape and markings when extended in flight. Tail shape, length, color, and banding may play a big part, too. At left are diagrams detailing the various parts of a bird—its topography—labeled with the scientific name likely to be found in the text of this book.

The main body of each entry is divided into three categories: Behavior, Habitat, and Local Sites. The **Behavior** section details certain characteristics to look or listen for in the field. Often a bird's behavioral characteristics are very closely related to its body type and field marks, such as in the case of woodpeckers, whose chisel-shaped bills, stiff tails, strong legs, and sharp claws enable them to spend most of their lives in an upright position, braced against a tree trunk. The **Habitat** section describes areas that are most likely to support the featured species. Preferred nesting locations of breeding birds are also included in many cases. The **Local Sites** section recommends specific refuges or parks where the featured bird is likely to be found. A section called **Field Notes** finishes each entry, and includes information such as plumage variations within a species; or it may introduce another species with which thefeatured bird is frequently confused. In the latter case, an additional drawing may be included to help in identification.

Finally, a caption underneath each of the photographs explains the season of the plumage pictured, as well as the age and gender, of the bird above. A key to using this informative guide and its range maps follows on the next two pages.

READING THE SPREAD

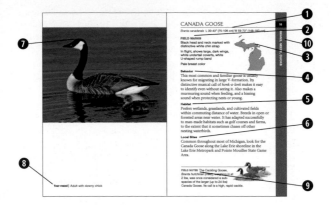

CANADA GOOSE

Branta canadensis L 30-43" (75-108 cm) W 50-73" (148-183 cm)

FIELD MARKS
Black head and neck marked with distinctive white chin strap

In flight, shows large, dark wings, white undertail coverts, white U-shaped rump band

Pale breast color

Behavior
This most common and familiar goose is usually known for migrating in large V-formation. Its distinctive musical call of *honk-a-lonk* makes it easy to identify even without seeing it. Also makes a murmuring sound when feeding, and a hissing sound when protecting nests or young.

Habitat
Prefers wetlands, grasslands, and cultivated fields within commuting distance of water. Breeds in open or forested areas near water. It has adapted successfully to man-made habitats such as golf courses and farms, to the extent that it sometimes chases off other nesting waterbirds.

Local Sites
Common throughout most of Michigan, look for the Canada Goose along the Lake Erie shoreline in the Lake Erie Metropark and Pointe Mouillee State Game Area.

FIELD NOTE The Cackling Goose, *Branta hutchinsii* (here), weighing in at 2 lbs, was once considered a sub-species of the larger (up to 24 lbs) Canada Goose. Its call is a high, rapid cackle.

Tear-round | Adult with downy chick

---

1 Heading: Beneath the Common Name find the Latin, or Scientific, Name. Beside it is the bird's length, and frequently wingspan. Wingspan occurs with birds often seen in flight. Female measurements are given if disparate from the male's.

2 Field Marks: Gives basic field identification for body size, head and bill shape, and markings.

3 Range Map: Shows year-round range in purple, breeding range in red, winter range in blue, migration areas in green, and breeding colonies by black dots.

4 Behavior: A step beyond **Field Marks**, gives clues to identifying a bird's habits, such as feeding, flight pattern, courtship, nest-building, and songs and calls.

5 Habitat: Reveals the area a species most likely inhabits, such as

forested regions, marshy areas, cities, or farms. May include preferred nesting sites.

6 Local Sites: Details local spots to look for a given species.

7 Photograph: Shows bird in its habitat. May be a female or male, adult or juvenile. Plumage is breeding, molting, or nonbreeding.

8 Caption: Defines the featured bird's plumage, age, and gender, as seen in the picture.

9 Field Note: A special entry that may give a unique point of identification, compare two species of the same family, compare two species from different families that are easily confused, or focus on a historic or conservation fact.

10 Band: Gives the common name of the bird's family.

On each map of Michigan, range boundaries are drawn where the species ceases to be regularly seen. Nearly every species will be rare at the edges of its range. The sample map shown below explains the colors and symbols used on each map. Ranges continually expand and contract, so the map is a tool, not a rule. Range information is based on actual sightings and therefore depends upon the number of knowledgeable and active birders in each area.

Map Key

Breeding range, generally in spring and summer

Winter range

Year-round range

Migration range

• Breeding colony

Sample Map: Common Goldeneye

READING THE INDEXES

There are two indexes at the back of the book. The first (page 260) is a **Color Index**, created for birders to make quick IDs in the field. In this index, birds are labeled by their predominant color: Mostly White, Mostly Black, etc. Note that a bird may have a head of a different color than its label states. That's because its body— the part most noticeable in the field—is the color labeled.

The **Alphabetical Index** (page 264) is by the bird's common name. Next to each entry is a check-off box. Most birders make lists of the birds they see. Some keep several lists, perhaps one of birds in a certain area and another of all the birds they've ever seen—a life list. Such lists enable birders to look back and remember their first sighting of an Indigo Bunting or a Downy Woodpecker.

Year-round | Adult

TUNDRA SWAN

Cygnus columbianus I 52" (132 cm)

FIELD MARKS

White overall

Black facial skin tapers to point in front of eye and forms "U" shape across forehead

Yellow spot in front of eye

Rounded head, bill slightly concave

Behavior

Social bird, often seen in large groups. Flies in large V- shaped wedges. Call is a loud, noisy, high-pitched whooping or yodeling. Note that juvenile's bill is grayish pink, and upperparts appear more gray.

Habitat

Nests on tundra or sheltered marshes. Winters in flocks on shallow ponds, lakes, or estuaries. Breeds in extreme northern coastal areas of North America.

Local Sites

More often seen during migration, the Tundra Swan is known to have a small wintering population on western Lake Erie. South of Detroit, Lake Erie Metropark is a good viewing location in winter.

FIELD NOTES The larger Trumpeter Swan, *Cygnus buccinator* (inset), has a straight bill, and black facial skin that comes to a broad point in front of the eye and slopes into a "V" on the forehead. The juvenile Trumpeter Swan (inset, left), has gray-brown plumage that is retained through its first spring.

Year-round | Adult with downy chick

CANADA GOOSE

Branta canadensis L 30-43" (75-108 cm) W 59-73" (148-183 cm)

FIELD MARKS
Black head and neck marked with
distinctive white chin strap

In flight, shows large, dark wings,
white undertail coverts, white
U-shaped rump band

Pale breast color

Behavior
This most common and familiar goose is usually
known for migrating in large V-formation. Its
distinctive musical call of *honk-a-lonk* makes it easy
to identify even without seeing it. Also makes a
murmuring sound when feeding, and a hissing
sound when protecting nests or young.

Habitat
Prefers wetlands, grasslands, and cultivated fields
within commuting distance of water. Breeds in open or
forested areas near water. It has adapted successfully
to man-made habitats such as golf courses and farms,
to the extent that it sometimes chases off other
nesting waterbirds.

Local Sites
Common throughout most of Michigan, look for the
Canada Goose along the Lake Erie shoreline in the Lake
Erie Metropark and Pointe Mouillee State Game Area.

FIELD NOTES The Cackling Goose,
Branta hutchinsii (inset), weighing in at
2 lbs, was once considered a subspecies of the larger (up to 24 lbs)
Canada Goose. Its call is a high, rapid cackle.

Year-round | Adult white morphs

SNOW GOOSE

Chen caerulescens l 35" (89 cm) W 45" (114 cm)

FIELD MARKS
White overall

Black primaries

Thick, serrated, pinkish bill with
black "grinning patch"

Behavior
Seen in small groups, especially during fall migration
from high Arctic breeding grounds. Flocks travel in
loose V's and long lines of loud, vocal birds, sounding
like baying hounds. Strong flyers, they attain speeds up
to 40 mph. Known to fly over 1,500 miles nonstop. Also
agile swimmers, often resting on water during
migration and in wintering grounds.

Habitat
Seen mainly in winter on grasslands, grainfields, and
wetlands, preferring standing shallow freshwater
marshes and flooded fields. Almost entirely vegetarian,
this goose forages on agricultural grains and plants and
on all parts of aquatic vegetation.

Local Sites
Uncommon and local throughout Michigan during
migration. Saginaw Bay and Allegan State
Game Area are best locations for sighting.

FIELD NOTES Look closely at individuals in a
flock and you may see the rare and diminutive
Ross's Goose, *Chen rossii* (inset), distinguished
by a short, stubby bill, a short neck, and a rounder head.

Breeding | Adult male

WOOD DUCK

Aix sponsa L 18¼" (47 cm)

FIELD MARKS

Distinctive glossy green plumage, large crest, reddish eye in male

Short crest, large white teardrop-shaped eye patch in female

Juvenile resembles female but is spotted below

Behavior

Most commonly feeds by picking insects from the water's surface or by tipping into shallows to pluck invertebrates from the bottom. Wood Duck hens are known to hatch up to eight eggs in abandoned nests, or "dump nests," where as many as two dozen "cold" eggs have been left behind. The omnivorous Wood Duck's diet changes throughout the year depending upon available foods and its need for particular proteins or minerals during migration, breeding, and molting.

Habitat

Prefers woodlands and forested swamps. Nests in tree cavities or man-made nest boxes. A perching duck, the Wood Duck can be spotted in trees. It is especially common in open woodlands near water.

Local Sites

Michigan is one of the primary breeding grounds for the Wood Duck. Look for it during spring and summer in Pointe Mouillee State Game Area.

FIELD NOTES Males make a soft, upslurred whistle when swimming. Female Wood Ducks have a distinctive rising, squealing flight call of *oo-eek*. Males molt to a drab eclipse plumage, but retain their distinctive white throat pattern and bill colors.

Breeding | Adult male

MALLARD

Anas platyrhynchos L 23" (58 cm)

FIELD MARKS

Male has metallic green head and neck; white collar; chestnut breast

Female is mottled brown; orange bill marked with black

Both have white tail, underwings; bright-blue speculum with both sides bordered in white

Behavior

A dabbler, the Mallard feeds by picking insects from the water's surface or by tipping into shallows and plucking invertebrates and grasses from the bottom. Male's courtship display includes dipping his bill into water and bringing it up smartly. The Mallard springs directly into flight with no running start to take off. Hybridizes with other species of dabbler, such as the Mottled Duck and the American Black Duck (below).

Habitat

A widespread duck, the Mallard prefers freshwater shallows and, in winter, salt marshes. The domestic Mallard copes well with man-made habitats. May be found feeding in marinas and breeding in backyards.

Local Sites

Common throughout Michigan year-round. Look for Mallards in any wetland throughout the state.

FIELD NOTES The American Black Duck, *Anas rubripes* (inset, bottom), occurs in much of the Mallard's eastern range. While the females of these two species are similar, the Black Duck is distinguished by an unmarked greenish yellow bill and a black-brown body. A Black Duck and Mallard hybrid (inset, top) has a chestnut breast and a green postocular stripe.

Breeding | Adult male

GREEN-WINGED TEAL

Anas crecca L 14½" (37 cm)

FIELD MARKS

Male's chestnut head has dark green ear patch outlined in buff

Female has smaller bill than that of other female teal; also white undertail coverts, mottled flanks

In flight, shows green speculum bordered in buff on leading edge

Behavior

An agile and fast-moving flier, this is the smallest species of duck known as dabblers. Dabblers either take food from the water's surface or upend, tail in the air and head submerged, to reach aquatic plants, seeds, and snails. The Green-winged has a specialized bill for filtering food from mud. Travels in small flocks that synchronize their midair twists and turns.

Habitat

In summer, prefers open country near shallow fresh-water lakes and marshes. Also found in coastal estuaries and tidal marshes, and on shallow lakes and ponds inland, especially those covered with standing or floating vegetation. Nests are hidden among grasses and weeds, within 200 feet of water.

Local Sites

Check Pointe Mouillee State Game Area and Muskegon Wastewater System during spring and fall migration.

FIELD NOTES The female Blue-winged Teal, *Anas discors* (inset, left), has a large bill, spotted undertail coverts, yellowish legs. The male's head is violet-gray, with a white crescent on either side.

Breeding | Adult male

AMERICAN WIGEON

Anas Americana L 19" (48 cm)

FIELD MARKS
Conspicuous white cap and fore-head on male; green patch extending back from eyes; white wing patch

Both sexes have mainly white wing linings

Rusty brown chest, white underparts

Behavior
Although a dabbling duck, the American Wigeon also grazes in fields and was once considered an agricultural pest. Often feeds in shallow water with other duck species; has also been known to forage in deeper waters, and to steal food from diving ducks.

Habitat
This freshwater bird may be found in various habitats, ranging from marshes to lakes, bays, coastal estuaries, and fields. The American Wigeon's shallow nest is built on dry land among tall weeds.

Local Sites
Widespread throughout Michigan, look for the American Wigeon in flocks mixed with other waterfowl along the shores of Saginaw Bay, particularly in the Nayanquing Point State Wildlife Area.

FIELD NOTES Compare the American Wigeon to the Gadwall, *Anas strepera*. The Gadwall male (inset, right) is mostly gray, with a white belly, black tail coverts, pale chestnut on wings. The female Gadwall (inset, left) has mottled brown plumage, and a gray upper mandible with orange sides.

Breeding | Adult male

NORTHERN PINTAIL

Anas acuta Male L 26" (66 cm), Female L 20" (51 cm)

FIELD MARKS
Bill is uniformly grayish

Male has chocolate brown head; long, slender white neck, with white extending to back of head

Male's black central tail feathers extend far beyond tail. Female mottled brown; paler head, neck

Behavior
This common, widespread duck is probably one of the most numerous duck species in the world. During courtship, several males may compete for the attention of one female, sometimes resulting in chases. Male's call is weak *geeee*; whistle, *prrrippp*.

Habitat
Forages in cut grainfields, especially in winter, nibbling or "mumbling" remnant corn from the cob. The Northern Pintail, a dabbler, is also commonly found in marshes and open areas with ponds and lakes, where it will tip into the water to search the underwater mud.

Local Sites
The Northern Pintail is found throughout the state during migration. St. Clair Flats State Wildlife Area and Saginaw Bay are likely locations.

FIELD NOTES Although widespread and abundant, the Northern Pintail tends to be a very secretive bird, particularly during its late summer molt. The young of this species leave the nest just hours after hatching and begin finding their own food, though their mother continues to tend to them.

Breeding | Adult male

CANVASBACK

Aythya valisineria L 21" (53 cm)

FIELD MARKS
Breeding male's head and neck
are chestnut, back and sides
whitish

Female's and eclipse male's head
and neck pale brown; back and
sides pale brown-gray

Forehead slopes to long, black bill

Behavior
Feeds on the water in large flocks by diving deep for
fish, mollusks, and marine vegetation. Its heavy body
requires a running start on water for takeoff. Flocks fly
fairly high in lines or in irregular V-formation. Walks
awkwardly, but not often seen on land. Listen for the
male's croak and the female's quack.

Habitat
Primarily occurs on the Great Lakes, with smaller numbers on inland lakes throughout the state.

Local Sites
Anchor Bay, Belle Isle Park in the Detroit River, and
the waters off Lake Erie Metropark are good locations from fall through spring.

FIELD NOTES Sharing the male Canvasback's reddish head and
neck and whitish back and sides, the male Redhead, *Aythya
americana* (inset), can be difficult to distinguish in the field. Look
for the tricolored bill of pale blue, white,
and black; and for the yellow, rather
than red, eyes. Redhead hens will
frequently deposit their eggs in the
nests of Canvasbacks.

Breeding | Adult male

LESSER SCAUP

Aythya affinis L 16½" (42 cm)

FIELD MARKS
Slight crown peak on black head, showing purple gloss in light

Black at tip of bill

Black neck and breast, black tail

Female has brown head, neck, upperparts; white at base of bill

Behavior
An omnivorous diving duck that forages on aquatic insects, mollusks, and crustaceans. Will dive to the bottom to sift through the mud while swimming. Also consumes snails, leeches, and small fish, and will forage for seeds and vegetation. Constructs nest near or above water and sometimes in upland environments, unlike any other diving duck.

Habitat
In winter will gather in large foraging flocks on ponds, lakes, rivers, and reservoirs, where it feeds mainly on mollusks, crustaceans, and insects.

Local Sites
The Lesser Scaup is migratory throughout Michigan, but look for it in Lake Erie Metropark and the southern portion of the state during winter months.

FIELD NOTES The Greater Scaup, *Aythya marila* (inset), closely resembles the Lesser in both sexes. The Greater's bill is larger, its head more smoothly rounded, and it has a longer white wing stripe, which shows in flight. The larger diver is seldom seen inland, instead flocking by the thousands along the coastlines of the Great Lakes.

Breeding | Adult male

COMMON GOLDENEYE

Bucephala clangula L 18¼" (47 cm)

FIELD MARKS
Triangular head brown in female; black with greenish tinge in male

Male has white patch between eye and bill; female has white neck ring

Male has black upperparts; female brownish gray

Behavior
A diving duck, may be seen foraging in flocks, often with much of the flock diving simultaneously for food. In flight, look for a distinctive white band on the secondaries of both the male and female, and listen for a whistling sound as they pass overhead.

Habitat
Prefers open lakes near woodlands where nest holes are available in large tree cavities. In winter, may retire in coastal areas or inland lakes and rivers. May sometimes use nest boxes or abandoned buildings for its nest, lining the depression with wood chips and down.

Local Sites
The Common Goldeneye makes the eastern Upper Peninsula its summer home, so look for it in Seney National Wildlife Refuge or Isle Royale National Park. In winter, large flocks can often be seen on the south ern Great Lakes, such as at Warren Dunes State Park on Lake Michigan.

FIELD NOTES The courtship display of the Common Goldeneye male consists of a ritualized head rocking: Resting the back of its head on its back, it thrusts its head forward, its neck dips down into the water, and its bill points up.

Breeding | Adult male

BUFFLEHEAD

Bucephala albeola L 13½" (34 cm)

FIELD MARKS
Small duck; large puffy head;
steep forehead; short bill

Male has large white
head patch; glossy black back

Female has brown head with small,
elongated white patches on each
side

Behavior
Often seen in small flocks, some ducks keeping watch
at the surface while others dive for aquatic insects,
snails, and small fish. Like all divers, its feet are set well
back on the body to swiftly propel it through the water.
Migrates at night, riding favorable air currents. Attains
speeds of about 40 mph. A truly monogamous duck
believed to stay with the same mate and faithfully
return to the same nesting site each season.

Habitat
In its boreal forest breeding grounds, this smallest
of the North American diving ducks nests almost
exclusively in cavities created by the Northern Flicker—
a nesting site so tiny that it is speculated to have
influenced the Bufflehead's own small size.

Local Sites
Winters on the southern Great Lakes. Look for migrating Bufflehead on Saginaw Bay.

FIELD NOTES The male Hooded Merganser,
Lophodytes cucullatus (inset), larger than
the Bufflehead, has brown sides and a
spikelike bill. Its white patch extends into its
crest, which is bordered in black when raised.

Breeding | Adult male, left; Adult female, right

COMMON MERGANSER

Mergus merganser L 25" (64 cm)

FIELD MARKS

Large duck with long, slim neck and hooked, red bill

White breast and sides, often tinged with pink

Female has chestnut, crested head with white chin

Behavior

The long, serrated bill of all mergansers helps them to catch fish, crustaceans, and aquatic insects. In flight, they show pointed wings and a distinctive profile: The head looks like a bump between a long neck and bill. When Common Merganser males take flight, look for the white patch on the upper surface of the entire inner wing, partially crossed by a single black bar.

Habitat

Nest near water in woodlands or sheltered coastal areas, usually in a large tree cavity, or in holes under tree roots or undercut banks.

Local Sites

The Common Merganser makes its summer home in the Upper Peninsula and northern edges of the Lower. Look for it at Seney National Wildlife Refuge in the Upper Peninsula. During migration, look on large bodies of water throughout the state.

FIELD NOTES Smaller than the Common Merganser, the male Red-breasted Merganser, *Mergus oornator* (inset, left), sports a shaggy double crest, white collar, streaked breast, and distinctive white shoulder patch. Young male mergansers resemble the adult female (inset, center and right) of their species.

Breeding | Adult male

RUDDY DUCK

Oxyura jamaicensis L 15" (38 cm)

FIELD MARK

Breeding male has large black head with bold white cheeks; bright blue bill

Rusty red body, long black tail

Female is dull brown overall; whitish cheek with single dark line

Behavior

Referred to as a "stiff-tail" for its long, spikey tail feathers which are often cocked up in the air. This chunky diver is noted for its grebelike ability to sink beneath the surface and disappear. Adapted for diving, it has the largest feet relative to body size of all ducks. With legs positioned far back on its body, it can barely walk upright. Feeds primarily on aquatic insects and crustaceans; eats little vegetable matter.

Habitat

Makes its nest in dense vegetation of freshwater wetlands, and may be found on lakes and bays during migration and winter.

Local Sites

The Ruddy Duck rarely winters in the extreme western and southern portions of the Lower Peninsula, and may be seen in the rest of the state during migration. Check the area along Saginaw Bay and the Muskegon Wastewater System for these seemingly lethargic waterfowl.

FIELD NOTES Unlike most ducks, pair bonds form after arrival at breeding grounds and seem to last only until incubation starts. Nests are usually constructed over water in emergent vegetation. Female lays largest eggs in relation to body size of all ducks.

Year-round | Adult male

RING-NECKED PHEASANT

Phasianus colchicus Male L 33" (84 cm) Female L 21" (53 cm)

FIELD MARKS
Long, pointed tail; short, rounded wings

Male iridescent bronze, mottled with black, brown, and green; female duller, buffy overall

Male has glossy head; fleshy red eye patches; iridescent ear tufts

Behavior

The Ring-necked Pheasant, like other game birds, feeds primarily on seeds and grains, but will also feed on weeds, buds, berries, and insects, depending upon availability. The male's territorial call is a loud, penetrating *kok-cack*, and both sexes will make hoarse, croaking alarm notes. When flushed, the pheasant rises almost vertically with a loud whirring of wings.

Habitat

Prefers open country, farmlands, brushy areas, or woodland edges.

Local Sites

A year-round resident of southern Michigan, look for the Ring-necked Pheasant while exploring trails in brushy areas in many of Michigan's state game areas.

FIELD NOTES The Ring-necked Pheasant was introduced to North America from Asia. It is generally a shy bird, and the female is especially difficult to spot in open country because of her cryptic plumage. Like other game birds, it has a crop that is used to store food, thus reducing the amount of time required for it to forage in the open. Strong, muscular legs, with a spiny spur or claw just above the male's hind toe, allow the Ring-necked to run and hide from danger, rather than to fly.

Year-round | Adult male

WILD TURKEY

Meleagris gallopavo L 37-46" (94-117 cm)

FIELD MARKS
Male has dark purple, green, and bronze plumage

Bald, red and blue head; fleshy red eye patches; red wattle

Male has black chest "beard"

Female smaller and browner

Behavior
A ground forager, the Wild Turkey is known to roost in trees at night. It can fly well for short distances, but prefers to walk or run. Male's characteristic display during breeding season involves puffing out its chest, swelling its wattles, spreading its tail, and rattling its wings, all while gobbling and strutting. Male gobbling call may be heard in spring from a mile away.

Habitat
Largest of game birds, but shy, the turkey lives communally in small family flocks. Frequents open forests and feeds on seeds, nuts, acorns, and insects found in grainfields and forest edges. Females raise large broods, nesting in leaf-lined hollows in brush or woodlands.

Local Sites
A year-round resident, mainly in the Lower Peninsula, look for the Wild Turkey in the woodlands of Waterloo State Recreation Area.

FIELD NOTES Up to 6,000 feathers cover the body of an adult Wild Turkey—in patterns called feather tracts—keeping it warm in winter months. Note that the feathery "beard" that develops on its chest and the spiney spurs on the back of its lower legs are characteristic of males only.

Year-round | Adult female gray morph

RUFFED GROUSE

Bonasa umbellus L 17" (43 cm)

FIELD MARKS
Brown overall, mottled with darker brown and white

Small crest

Black ruffs on neck, usually inconspicuous; multibanded tail

Wide, dark band near tip of tail

Behavior
In spring, the male attracts females to his territory by raising the black ruffs at the sides of his neck, fanning his tail, and beating his wings to make a hollow, accelerating, drumming noise. Flushed birds burst into flight with a roar of wings.

Habitat
A woodland bird that prefers deciduous or mixed forests with brushy cover, the Ruffed Grouse can also be seen near forest clearings. Though it prefers plant material and seeds, its diet varies by season and can include insects, small reptiles, and amphibians

Local Sites
The most common grouse in North America; a year-round resident of the entire state of Michigan. Check the wooded areas of Hartwick Pines State Park for these game birds.

FIELD NOTES Note the chestnut tip on the black tail of the Spruce Grouse, *Falcipennis canadensis* (inset). In Michigan, Spruce Grouse are restricted to patches of boreal forest. The female is similar in appearance to the Ruffed Grouse, but lacks the small crest and black ruffs on the neck.

Breeding | Adult

COMMON LOON

Gavia immer L 32" (81 cm)

FIELD MARKS
White-checked plumage, black
bill during breeding

Steep forehead, peaked crown

Dark crown and nape, white on
lower face and breast in winter

Behavior
A diving bird. Prefers fish up to ten inches long, which
it harpoons with its pointed beak. While swimming,
keeps head level at all times. Forages by diving and
swimming underwater, propelled mainly by large,
paddle-shaped feet. Can stay submerged for up to
three minutes at depths of up to 250 feet. It is nearly
impossible for the Common Loon to walk on land.
Its loud yodeling call may be heard year-round, most
often on breeding grounds in spring and summer.

Habitat
Nests on large wooded lakes. Winters in coastal waters,
or inland on large, ice-free bodies of water with ample
room for takeoff.

Local Sites
In summer, look for Common Loons in Pigeon River
State Forest or, in the Upper Peninsula, at Seney
National Wildlife Reserve.

FIELD NOTES The related Red-throated
Loon, *Gavia stellata* (inset), has a gray
head, slightly upturned bill, and
tends to hold its head tilted up, The
breeding adult has a brick red throat patch that is dark in flight.
Winter adult has a sharply defined white face and extensive
white spotting on its back.

Breeding | Adult

PIED-BILLED GREBE

Podilymbus podiceps L 13½" (34 cm)

FIELD MARKS
Short-necked, big-headed, stocky

Breeding adult brown overall;
black ring around stout, whitish bill;
black chin and throat

Winter birds lose bill ring,
chin becomes white

Behavior
The most secretive yet most common of North American grebes, the Pied-billed is seldom seen on land or in flight. When alarmed, it slowly sinks into the water, holding only its head above the surface. Its strong, stout bill allows it to feed on hard-shelled crustaceans, breaking apart and crushing the shells with ease. Like most grebes, it eats feathers and feeds them to its young, perhaps to protect the stomach lining from fish bones.

Habitat
Prefers nesting around freshwater marshes and ponds. Also found in more open waters of large bays and rivers, where it dives to feed on aquatic insects, small fish, frogs, and vegetable matter. Found in all of the lower 48 states.

Local Sites
The Pied-billed Grebe makes its summer home throughout Michigan. Look for it in the Maple River State Game Area.

FIELD NOTES Often compared to loons because of their superb diving abilities, there are seven species of grebe in North America. Lobed toes make them strong swimmers.

Immature

DOUBLE-CRESTED CORMORANT

Phalacrocorax auritus L 32" (81 cm) W 52" (132 cm)

FIELD MARKS
Large, rounded throat pouch,
yellow-orange year-round

Bill hooked at tip

Immature has pale breast

Distinctive kinked neck when flying

Behavior
After locating prey at surface, dives to considerable
depths, propelling itself with legs and fully webbed feet.
Uses its hooked bill to grasp fish. When it leaves the
water, it perches on a dock or piling and half-spreads
its wings to dry. Feeds on a variety of aquatic animals
and plants. May soar briefly at times, its neck in an
S-shape. May swim submerged to the neck.

Habitat
Common and widespread, the Double-crested
Cormorant may be found along coasts, inland lakes,
and rivers. The most numerous and far-ranging of
North American cormorants, it adapts to fresh- or
saltwater environments.

Local Sites
During summer months, look for the Double-
crested Cormorant along the Straits of Mackinac
and Saginaw Bay. During migration, it can be found
mainly along Great Lakes shorelines.

FIELD NOTES Despite its name, the crests on the head of the
breeding Double-crested Cormorant are rarely seen in the field,
especially in the case of the eastern breeding adult, whose
crests are black and less conspicuous than the white crests of
the western breeding adult. Juvenile birds are brownish above,
and pale below, particularly on the breast and neck.

Breeding | Adult

GREAT EGRET

Ardea alba L 39" (99 cm) W 51" (130 cm)

FIELD MARKS

Large white heron with heavy yellow bill, black legs and feet

Breeding adult has long plumes trailing from its back, extending beyond the tail

Duller bill and legs in nonbreeding adults and juveniles

Behavior

Stalks its prey slowly and methodically, foraging in shallow water with sharply pointed bill for small fish, aquatic insects, frogs, and crayfish. Also known to hunt snakes, birds, and small mammals. May forage in groups or steal food from smaller birds.

Habitat

Common to wetlands. The Great Egret makes its nest in trees or shrubs between 10 and 40 feet above the ground. Colonies may have a hundred birds. Occasionally breeds as far north as Canada.

Local Sites

The Pointe Mouillee State Game Area is a favorite hangout of this wader. There is also a Great Egret rookery in Island Lake, near the West Bloomfield Nature Area. Post-breeding birds wander as far north as the Straits of Mackinac.

FIELD NOTES Early in the breeding season, the Great Egret grows long, ostentatious feathers called aigrettes, and it is from this word that the common name "egret" is derived. In the late 1800s, the millinery industry used aigrettes so extensively that Great Egrets were hunted nearly to extinction. The campaign to end this trend became the National Audubon Society, and the Great Egret remains the symbol of the Society today.

Immature

GREAT BLUE HERON

Ardea herodias L 46" (117 cm) W 72" (183 cm)

FIELD MARKS
Gray-blue heron, white foreneck
with black streaks

Black stripe extends above eye

Breeding adult has dull yellow bill
and ornate plumes on head

Juvenile has dark crown, no plumes

Behavior
Often seen standing or wading along calm coastlines or
rivers, foraging for food; or flying high, its head folded
back onto its shoulders. Emits an annoyed, deep,
guttural squawk as it takes flight. When threatened,
draws back its neck, erects its plumes, and points its bill
at opponent.

Habitat
May be seen hunting for aquatic creatures and,
occasionally, snakes and insects in marshes, shores, and
swamps. Farther from water, Great Blues can also be
found hunting mice and small woodchucks in farm
fields, meadows, and forest edges. Pairs of Great Blues
build large stick nests high in trees in loose association.
These "heronries" are sometimes miles from water.

Local Sites
The largest and most familiar heron in North America,
look for the Great Blue throughout Michigan's
wetlands and fields.

FIELD NOTES The name "crane" is often
mistakenly applied to the Great Blue
Heron, but cranes belong to a different family.
The Sandhill Crane, *Grus canadensis* (inset),
sometimes shares the Great Blue Heron's territory;
note the patch of red skin on its crown and lores.

Year-round | Adult

GREEN HERON

Butorides virescens L 18" (46 cm) W 26" (66 cm)

FIELD MARKS

Small, chunky; short, yellow legs

Greenish black crown feathers, sometimes a shaggy crest

Deep chestnut neck, green and blue-gray above, white center of throat and neck in adult

Behavior

Usually solitary, this heron's common cry of *kyowk* may be heard as it flies away. It stands at the edge of shallow water and tosses twigs, insects, even earthworms into the water as lures to attract minnows. The Green Heron spends most of its day in the shade. When alarmed, it may make a show by flicking its tail, raising its crest, elongating its neck and, in the process, revealing its streaked throat plumage.

Habitat

Found in a variety of habitats but prefers streams, ponds, and marshes with woodland cover. Often perches in trees.

Local Sites

The solitary Green Heron is found in wetlands throughout southern Michigan during breeding season. Maple River State Game Area is an especially likely place to find the heron.

FIELD NOTES In one of the few instances of tool use in the bird world, the Green Heron creates its own lures to attract minnows, breaking off twigs and tossing them into the water. This heron also uses live bait, digging up earthworms or catching insects and using them to capture its food. It has also been known to put bread or popcorn to the same use.

Year-round | Adult

BLACK-CROWNED NIGHT-HERON

Nycticorax nycticorax L 25" (64 cm) W 44" (112 cm)

FIELD MARKS

Black crown and back; red eyes

Two to three white hindneck plumes, longest when breeding

White underparts and face

Gray wings, tail, and sides of neck

Behavior

Primarily a night feeder. Even when feeding during daylight hours, remains in the shadows, almost motionless, waiting for prey to come within range. Forages on fish, frogs, rodents, snakes, lizards, mollusks, bird eggs, and baby birds. Black-crowneds are high on the food chain and susceptible to accumulating contaminants, so their population status is an indicator of our environmental quality.

Habitat

This heron has adapted to a wide range of habitats, including freshwater wetlands and lakeshores that provide cover and forage, along with reservoirs and flooded agricultural fields.

Local Sites

The Pointe Mouillee State Game Area, an extensive area of natural wetlands and diked marshes at the mouth of the Huron River, is a good location to spot this wader. Post-breeding birds wander as far north as the Straits of Mackinac.

FIELD NOTES The Black-crowned Night-Heron will not distinguish between its young and those belonging to other Night-Herons, and will care for other broods.

Year-round | Adult

TURKEY VULTURE

Cathartes aura L 27" (69 cm) W 69" (175 cm)

FIELD MARKS
Naked red head; ivory bill;
red legs

Brownish black feathers over
body; silver-gray flight feathers

In flight, contrasting underwings
show and long tail extends
beyond feet

Behavior
An excellent flier, the Turkey Vulture soars high above
the ground in search of carrion and refuse, watching
for other scavengers. Rocks from side to side in flight,
seldom flapping its wings, which are held upward in a
shallow V, allowing it to gain lift from conditions that
would deter many other raptors. Feeds heavily when
food is available but can go days without if necessary.

Habitat
Hunts in open country, woodlands, farms, even in
urban dumps and landfills. Nests solitarily in hollow
logs or, less frequently, in hollow trees, crevices, caves,
mine shafts. Spread of Turkey Vultures in the Northeast
is considered a result of increased number of white-
tailed deer and, consequently, increased roadkills.

Local Sites
Widespread throughout the state during breeding season. At the peak of migration in October, look for
hundreds of vultures circling together high in the air.

FIELD NOTES The most widespread vulture in North America,
popularly known as a "buzzard," the Turkey Vulture's naked head
is an adaptation that keeps it from soiling its feathers while feeding and reduces the risk of picking up disease from carcasses. It
also has an unusually well-developed sense of smell, allowing it
to locate carrion concealed in forest settings.

Year-round | Adult

OSPREY

Pandion haliaetus L 22-25" (56-64 cm) W 58-72" (147-183 cm)

FIELD MARKS

Dark brown above, white below

White head, with prominent dark eye stripe

Gray beak

Females have darker streaking on neck

Behavior

Hunts by soaring over water, hovering, then diving down and plunging feet first into water to snatch its prey with specialized barbs on its toes. Feeds only on fish. Call is a series of clear, resonant, whistled *kyews*, which herald the arrival of spring. The Osprey also uses its call during breeding season to draw a female's attention to a prized fish hooked in its talons.

Habitat

Vacates most of North America after breeding season yet returns early from wintering grounds in Central and South America. Nests near bodies of freshwater. Its large, bulky nests are built in trees or on poles, docks, or specialized man-made platforms. Uncommon inland yet found on all continents except Antarctica.

Local Sites

Watch Michigan's lakeshores for this raptor, especially at Lake Erie Metropark in migration.

FIELD NOTES Female Ospreys tend to be larger than males. Both parents brood; however, females do the majority of brooding while the male hunts and brings her food. Both parents feed their hatchlings.

Year-round | Female

NORTHERN HARRIER

Circus cyaneus L 17-23" (43-58 cm) W 38-48" (97-122 cm)

FIELD MARKS
Owl-like facial disk

Slim body; long, narrow wings
with rounded tips; long tail

Adult male gray above, whitish
below; female brown above,
whitish below, with brown streaks
on breast and flanks

Behavior

Harriers generally perch low and fly close to the
ground, wings upraised, as they search for birds, mice,
frogs, and other prey. They seldom soar high except
during migration and in exuberant, acrobatic courtship
display, during which the male loops and somersaults
in the air. Often found hunting in the dim of dawn or
dusk, using their well-developed hearing. Identifiable
by a thin, insistent whistle.

Habitat

Once called the Marsh Hawk, this harrier can be found
in wetlands and open country. Nests invariably on the
ground. During winter months, roosts comunally on
the ground.

Local Sites

The lower half of Michigan is home to the Northern
Harrier year-round. It may be found in the rest of the
state during the summer breeding season. Look for this
raptor in Seney National Wildlife Refuge.

FIELD NOTES Take care when attempting to identify a Northern
Harrier high overhead. It can look like a falcon when gliding, due
to its long, broad tail; or like an accipiter when soaring, due to
the rounded tips of its wings. Look for its bright white rump, one
of the most noticeable field marks of any hawk.

Year-round | Adult, left; Third-year, right

BALD EAGLE

Haliaeetus leucocephalus L 31-37" (79-94 cm) W 70-90" (178-229 cm)

FIELD MARKS
Distinctive white head and tail

Large yellow beak, feet, and eyes

Brown body

Juveniles mostly dark, showing
blotchy white on underwing
and tail

Behavior
Rock-steady flier, rarely swerving or tipping on its
flattened wings as a Turkey Vulture will do. Feeds
mainly on fish, but often on carrion and injured
squirrels, rabbits, and muskrats as well. Sometimes
steals fish from other birds of prey. Bald Eagles lock
talons and cartwheel together through the sky in an
elaborate dance during courtship.

Habitat
A member of the sea-eagle group; most often lives and
feeds along seacoasts or along rivers and lakes. Known
to perch in tall trees or on sandbars of rivers rich in
salmon. The Bald Eagle will nest solitarily in tall trees
or on cliffs.

Local Sites
The Bald Eagle's year-round range includes most of the
northern part of Michigan. Good sites include Seney
National Wildlife Refuge; and, in winter, the western
shore of Lake Erie.

FIELD NOTES The Bald Eagle's nest is characterized by a
collection of sticks lined with finer materials, high in a tree or in a
cliff's crevice. Making great strides in recovery after pesticide
bans, the Bald Eagle population is most abundant in Alaska, and
has been moved from endangered to threatened status.

Juvenile

COOPER'S HAWK

Accipiter cooperii L 14-20" (36-51 cm) W 29-37" (74-94 cm)

FIELD MARKS

Dark gray to black cap; bright red to yellow eyes, yellow base of bill

Blue-gray upperparts

Reddish bars across breast, belly

Long, rounded, barred tail with white terminal band

Behavior

Usually scans for prey from a perch, then attacks with a sudden burst of speed. Also flies fast and close to the ground, using brush to conceal its rapid attack. Will scan for prey while soaring. Typically feeds on birds, rabbits, rodents, reptiles, and insects. Known to hold prey underwater to drown it. Usually consumes prey by eating it head first, then entrails, and finally muscles.

Habitat

Prefers broken, especially deciduous, woodlands and streamside groves. Has adapted to fragmented woodlands created by urban and suburban development. Frequently found in larger trees in urban woods and parks.

Local Sites

Lake Erie Metropark, south of Detroit, is a good spot for watching raptors, including the Cooper's Hawk, during fall migration; especially on days with wind from the north or northwest.

FIELD NOTES Distinguished from Cooper's Hawk by a shorter, squared tail, thinner legs, and by a proportionately smaller head and neck, the Sharp-shinned Hawk, *Accipiter striatus* (inset), also lacks the Cooper's strong contrast between crown and back.

Juvenile

RED-TAILED HAWK

Buteo jamaicensis L 22" (56 cm) W 50" (127 cm)

FIELD MARKS
Brown body, heavy beak; distinctive red tail

Whitish belly with dark streaks

Dark bar on leading edge of underwing

Juvenile has banded tail

Behavior
While searching for food, the Red-tailed Hawk hovers in place, sometimes kiting, or hanging motionless in the wind, as it scours the land, preying on rodents. Its distinctive call is a harsh, descending *keeeeeer*.

Habitat
Variable habitat, from woods with nearby open lands to plains and prairie groves. Scan for hawks along edges where fields meet forests, or where wetlands meet woodlands—favored habitats due to the variety of prey found there.

Local Sites
The Red-tailed Hawk makes its home year round throughout the state. It is the most commonly seen roadside raptor in Michigan.

FIELD NOTES The related Red-shouldered Hawk, *Buteo lineatus* (inset), is a slightly smaller bird. It has spotted brown plumage with reddish shoulders, wing linings, and chest; and a long tail with broad white tail bands.

Year-round | Male

AMERICAN KESTREL

Falco sparverius L 10½" (27 cm) W 23" (58 cm)

FIELD MARKS
Russet back and tail

Two black stripes on white face

Male has blue-gray wing coverts,
and row of white spots on trailing
edge of wing

Female has russet wing coverts

Behavior
Feeds on insects, reptiles, mice, and other small
mammals, often hovering over prey before plunging.
Will also feed on small birds, especially in winter
Regularly seen perched on telephone lines, frequently
bobbing its tail. Has clear call of *killy-killy-killy*.

Habitat
The most widely distributed falcon, the American
Kestrel is commonly seen in open country and in cities.
Can often be found mousing along highway medians
or sweeping down the lakeshore.

Local Sites
This smallest and most common of our falcons may be
found throughout the state during summer breeding
season; good numbers can be seen in migration at
lakeside areas such as Lake Erie Metropark.

FIELD NOTES A related species, the Merlin,
Falco columbarius, is slightly larger than the
American Kestrel, with broader wings, and lack-
ing the Kestrel's strong facial markings. Note
female's dark brown upperparts, and male's
gray-blue plumage (inset; right, left).

Year-round | Adult

PEREGRINE FALCON

Falco peregrinus L 16-20" (41-51 cm) W 36-44" (91-112 cm)

FIELD MARKS

Crown and nape black

Black extends below eye, forming distinctive "helmet"

Adult shows rufous wash below

Juvenile is brownish above; underparts heavily streaked

Behavior

Hunts by flying high, swooping in on prey in a spectactular dive, or by flying low over the water, surprising the prey. Feeds primarily on birds; the larger of which may be knocked out of the air, and subsequently eaten on the ground.

Habitat

Inhabits open wetlands near cliffs; now is also well established in cities, nesting on bridges or on tall buildings. Nest usually nothing more than a scrape, with a few sticks or decorative foliage added. Nest sites may be used for many years. Though Peregrines will tenaciously defend their nest during breeding season, they hunt a much wider area.

Local Sites

The Peregrine may be seen throughout the state during migration. At Tawas Point State Park, take the Sandy Hook Nature Trail and watch for a Peregrine swooping down the shore line.

FIELD NOTES Use of pesticides such as DDT greatly reduced the number of Peregrine Falcons in the mid 1900s, but the species is making a strong comeback in areas where it has been reintroduced. Still, it is considered threatened and vigilant efforts are required to ensure the Peregrine Falcon's survival.

Year-round | Adult

VIRGINIA RAIL

Rallus limicola L 9½" (24 cm)

FIELD MARKS
Small, reddish overall

Gray cheeks

Reddish, slightly decurved bill

Reddish legs

Flanks black with white streaks

Behavior
Forages on ground for small aquatic invertebrates, including snails, spiders, beetles, and larvae. Uses its long, decurved bill to probe in silt and the damp floor of marsh vegetation. Will climb reeds and grass stalks in pursuit of insects and snails. Extremely long toes allow the rail to walk on floating marsh vegetation; strong legs help it to run and disappear into the marsh to avoid predators. Rails prefer running to flying.

Habitat
Inhabits freshwater marshes and wetlands. Nests are built low to the ground, even slightly into water, and are very difficult to find.

Local Sites
During breeding season, find the Virginia Rail in Nayanquing State Wildlife Area, or the Pointe Mouillee State Game Area.

FIELD NOTES Rails are strong runners, but weak fliers with poorly developed flight muscles. Their short, rounded wings mean they travel with rapid wing beats and fly for short distances, then abruptly drop—rather ungracefully—to the ground, where they instantly run to cover. Though the Virginia Rail is a game bird in most states, it is so secretive few are taken by hunters. Continual loss of habitat is the main threat to this species.

Breeding | Adult

SORA

Porzana carolina L 8¾" (22 cm)

FIELD MARKS
Short, thick yellow or greenish-yellow bill

Breeding adult is coarsely streaked above; face and center of throat and breast are black

In winter, black throat is somewhat obscured by gray edgings

Behavior
Forages on the ground or in the mud and water for seeds, insects, snails, and other aquatic invertebrates. Its call, heard year-round, includes a descending whinny and a sharp, high-pitched *keek*. During breeding seaon, a whistled *ker-wheer* is heard.

Habitat
The Sora prefers freshwater marshes, but may be seen in wet meadows or other wetlands while foraging. Its nest consists of a well-built cup of grasses and cattails lined with finer grasses in dense marsh brush, a few inches above the water.

Local Sites
The Sora is very secretive, and is more often heard than seen. Close attention in wetlands in Pointe Mouillee State Game Area may reveal this rail.

FIELD NOTES Compare the Sora with the rare and threatened Yellow Rail, *Coturnicops noveboracensis* (inset). Note the deep tawny yellow above, with wide dark stripes. In flight, the Yellow Rail shows a large white patch on the trailing edges of the wings. The juvenile Sora is not as black above, and its upperparts are streaked.

Year-round | Adult

AMERICAN COOT

Fulica americana L 15½" (39 cm)

FIELD MARKS

Blackish head and neck

Small, reddish brown forehead

Whitish bill with dark band at tip

Slate body

Outer feathers of undertail coverts white, inner ones black

Behavior

The distinctive toes of the American Coot are flexible and lobed, permitting it to swim well in open water and even dive in pursuit of aquatic vegetation beneath the surface. It has the ability to dive and stay submerged to feed. It bobs its head back and forth like a chicken when walking or swimming, and may be seen foraging in large flocks, especially during the winter. Note leg color, which ranges from green in juveniles to yellow in adults.

Habitat

Nests in freshwater marshes, in wetlands, or near lakes and ponds. Has also adapted well to human-altered habitats, including sewage lagoons, for foraging.

Local Sites

The American Coot is most readily sighted between late March and May in southern portions of the Lower Peninsula. Watch for coots in marshy areas in Pointe Mouillee State Game Area or Saginaw Bay.

FIELD NOTES The American Coot will build a floating nest, made of dead stems, lined with other material, and anchored to aquatic vegetation, in which it will generally lay six eggs each year.

Year-round | Adult with chicks

SANDHILL CRANE

Grus canadensis L 34-48" (86-122 cm) W 73-90" (185-229 cm)

FIELD MARKS

Plumage is gray overall

Dull red skin on crown and lores

Whitish chin, cheeks, and upper throat

Black primaries

Juvenile lacks red patch

Behavior

Stands with body horizontal, picking grain, seed, fruit, insects, and small vertebrates from surface of wetlands or farm fields. Call is a loud, trumpeting *gui-oo oo*, delivered frequently and intensely during courtship displays. Courtship consists of standardized movements of head, neck, and wings, paired with frenzied leaps resembling ballet moves. Preens itself with a muddy bill, staining the feathers of the upper back, lower neck, and breast.

Habitat

Breeds on grasslands and in marshes, building mounds of moist vegetation for nests.

Local Sites

Seney National Wildlife Refuge, Arcadia Marsh, Baker Sanctuary, and the Phyllis Haehnle Sanctuary are popular viewing spots for the Sandhill Crane.

FIELD NOTES Sandhill Cranes can live up to 20 years, and don't breed until they are at least two or three years old. Mated pairs remain together year-round and migrate as a family unit. Although the Sandhill Crane is not considered threatened, several of its subspecies are endangered: the race nesting in Cuba and the race that nests in coastal Mississippi.

Breeding | Adult

BLACK-BELLIED PLOVER

Pluvialis squatarola L 11½" (29 cm)

FIELD MARKS
Roundish head and body; large
eyes; short, dark bill; dark legs

Mottled gray, white belly in winter
and in juveniles

Breeding adult has frosted cap,
black and white spots on back
and wings

Behavior
Like other species of plover, this wary shorebird hunts in
small, loose groups for invertebrates such as worms,
shrimp, insects, eggs, and small crabs. Sometimes eats
berries. The plover locates its prey by sight, darts across
the ground, stops, then runs off again. When it does fly,
the Black-bellied Plover can be identified by a barred
white tail, white uppertail coverts, and black axillaries.

Habitat
This shorebird prefers sandy shores and beaches; less
common in interior regions away from the Great Lakes.
Nests on the Arctic tundra.

Local Sites
The Black-bellied Plover is a fairly common migrant
around the Great Lakes.

FIELD NOTES The Black-bellied is the only plover species in North
America that has a hind toe on its foot. Listen for its drawn-out,
three-note whistle, *pee-o-wee*; the second note is lower-pitched
than the other two. Note that the juvenile of this species may be
gold-speckled above, and a nonbreeding adult is paler gray
overall, with a white belly.

Juvenile

SEMIPALMATED PLOVER

Charadrius semipalmatus L 7¼" (18 cm)

FIELD MARKS
Dark brown back and breast
band; white eyebrow, chin, forehead patch and underparts

Breeding males have orangish eye
ring, may lack white eyebrow

Juveniles have darker legs; pale
fringed upperparts

Behavior
Feeds on aquatic worms, small mollusks, small
crustaceans, and eggs of aquatic animals. At very close
range, note the partial webbing between the toes. Call is
a whistled, upslurred *chu-weet*, and song is a series of
the same.

Habitat
Beaches, lakeshores, and mudflats are the preferred
habitat of the Semipalmated Plover, but it will make its
way inland during migration, visiting flooded fields.

Local Sites
Look for the Semipalmated Plover at Pointe Mouillee
State Game Area.

FIELD NOTES Compare the Piping Plover, *Charadrius melodus*
(inset), with the Semipalmated Plover. Note the paler buff
upperparts and brighter orange legs of the
Piping Plover. Its breeding plumage
includes a full or partial breast band.
The species has endangered status:
In 2004, 55 breeding pairs were found
in Michigan.

Year-round | Adult

KILLDEER

Charadrius vociferus L 10½" (27 cm)

FIELD MARKS

Tan to chocolate brown above, white neck and belly

Black double breast bands

Black stripe on forehead and extending back from black bill

Reddish eye ring

Behavior

Well-known for feigning a broken wing when predators come near its nest, it will limp to one side, drag its wing, and spread its tail. Once intruders are away from the nest, the instantly healed Killdeer will take flight and can then be identified by its reddish orange rump. Often seen running, then stopping on a dime with an inquisitive look, then suddenly jabbing at the ground with its bill. May gather in loose flocks. Feeds mainly on insects that live in short vegetation.

Habitat

Although a type of plover, the Killdeer generally prefers interior grassy regions, but may also be found on shores. In summer, it can be found across the entire continent of North America south of the tundra. Builds nest on open ground, usually on gravel.

Local Sites

The Killdeer may be seen on gravel rooftops or drive-ways throughout the state from March through November.

FIELD NOTES The Killdeer's loud, piercing, eponymous call of *kill-dee* or its ascending *dee-dee-dee* is often the signal for identifying these birds before sighting them. Listen also for a long, trilled *trrrrrrr* during courtship displays or when a nest is threatened by a predator.

Molting | Adult

GREATER YELLOWLEGS

Tringa melanoleuca L 14" (36 cm)

FIELD MARKS
Long, bright yellow legs

Long, dark, slightly upturned bill

Long, slender neck

White-speckled, gray-brown back

White underparts

Behavior
Observed alone or in small groups, this wary bird sounds an alarm when a hawk or falcon approaches. Call is distinctive series of three or more descending *tew-tew-tew* sounds. A forager of snails, crabs, and shrimp; also skims water surface for insects and larvae. Sprints short distances in pursuit of small fish.

Habitat
Breeds throughout the Canadian boreal zone, then winters throughout coastal North America and south into Mexico, utilizing a full range of wetlands, including marshes, ponds, lakes, rivers, and reservoirs.

Local Sites
In spring and fall migration, watch the prime waterfowl migration areas such as Pointe Mouillee State Game Area for this wader.

FIELD NOTES The Lesser Yellowlegs, *Tringa flavipes* (inset, left to right: juvenile, winter, breeding), is distinguished by its smaller size and shorter bill. The Lesser's call is often a single or double *tew*.

Breeding | Adult

SPOTTED SANDPIPER

Actitis macularia L 7½" (19 cm)

FIELD MARKS
Brown upperparts, barred during breeding season

White underparts, spotted brown during breeding

Tail shorter than other sandpipers

Short white wing stripe

Behavior
The somewhat larger female is the first to establish territory and defend it during breeding season. She may also mate with several males in a season. Males will tend to the eggs and young. Feeds on insects or crustaceans and other invertebrates by plucking them from the water's surface or even snatching them from the air. Walks with a nodding or teetering motion from birth.

Habitat
One of the most common and widespread sandpipers in North America during breeding season, preferring sheltered ponds, lakes, streams, or marshes.

Local Sites
Most common in summer in the Lower Peninsula; search at the Muskegon Wastewater System or Pointe Mouillee State Game Area.

FIELD NOTES Note the song of the Solitary Sandpiper, *Tringa solitaria* (inset), a higher pitched *peet-weet* than that of the Spotted Sandpiper. The Solitary Sandpiper has a longer neck, and its brown upperparts are heavily spotted buffy white. Its lower throat, breast, and sides are streaked blackish brown, and it displays a bold white eye ring. This sandpiper will often bob its tail while on the ground.

Year-round | Adult

UPLAND SANDPIPER

Bartramia longicauda L 12" (31 cm)

FIELD MARKS
Small head with large, dark eyes

Long, thin neck and bill

Long tail and wings

Mottled brown upperparts contrast with black primaries in flight

Yellow legs

Behavior
Moves through grass while foraging for a variety of seeds, insects, and other invertebrates. Calls include a rolling *pulip-pulip*; or another that sounds like a wolf whistle which it uses in flight during breeding season.

Habitat
Although classified among shorebirds, the Upland Sandpiper prefers grasslands, prairies, and fields, often where only its head is visible above the grass. Its numbers have declined from loss of habitat, but it was once very common in the Great Plains.

Local Sites
Look for this lanky sandpiper in grassy areas, sometimes near airports, paying special attention in the northern part of the Lower Peninsula and the Upper Peninsula. Visits to grasslands around Petoskey may yield some sightings.

FIELD NOTES When building a nest, the Upland Sandpiper may scrape out several depressions in the ground, but will only use one for its actual nest. It is known to spend up to eight months of the year in South America, its winter home.

Year-round | Adult

AMERICAN WOODCOCK

Scolopax minor L 11" (28 cm)

FIELD MARKS
Chunky, mottled brown body above
with lighter brown below

Long, stout bill

Short neck; short legs

Large eyes set high in the head

Rounded wings

Behavior

This secretive bird is most often spotted at dusk. Usually its nasal *peent* is heard before it is actually seen. It uses its long bill to probe deep into the damp earth on the forest floor for its favorite meal of earthworms. Will eat millipedes, beetles, and flies as well. Its upper bill is flexible, allowing it to snatch prey below ground. Flushed, it will fly up abruptly, its wings making a twittering sound.

Habitat

Although a shorebird, the American Woodcock prefers moist woodlands, where it roosts on the forest floor.

Local Sites

Favors openings in aspen and alder forests in the northern part of Michigan. Watch the ground carefully for this well-camouflaged bird in Manistee National Forest.

FIELD NOTES The slightly smaller Wilson's Snipe, *Gallinago delinata* (inset), has a long bill for probing, but prefers wetlands It has a boldly striped head and barred flanks. In swooping display flights, vibrating outer tail feathers make quavering hoots.

Breeding | Adult

BONAPARTE'S GULL

Larus philadelphia L 13½" (34 cm) W 33" (84 cm)

FIELD MARKS
Black bill; gray mantle

Breeding adult has black hood, absent in winter adult

Black-and-white wingtips, pale on underside; white underparts

Orange-red legs

Behavior

Among the smallest of North American gulls, it breeds in northern coniferous forests. Mainly nests in trees, one of the only gulls to do so. Constructs cup nest of twigs and bark lined with moss and lichens. Feeds on insects during breeding season. Favors marine environment during winter; often forages in large flocks.

Habitat

Common along the Great Lakes shoreline during migration, sometimes feeding several miles offshore. Will gather at river mouths, feeding on small fish and fish eggs.

Local Sites

Common during migration along Great Lakes coastlines in the southern part of the state, including Saginaw Bay and Muskegon.

FIELD NOTES Named after Charles Lucien Bonaparte, a nephew of Napoleon, the Bonaparte's Gull is one of the most graceful gulls in flight. A ferocious defender of its nest, it will assault intruders, including humans. Though it is omnivorous and willing to forage on a variety of prey, it seldom feeds at garbage dumps, unlike most other gulls.

Nonbreeding | Adult

RING-BILLED GULL

Larus dolawarensis L 17½" (45 cm) W 48" (122 cm)

FIELD MARKS
Yellow bill with black subterminal ring; yellowish legs

Pale eye with red orbital ring

Black primaries have white spots

Pale gray upperparts, white underparts

Behavior

This vocal gull is heard calling to other gulls, almost incessantly, especially during feeding and nesting. The call consists of a series of laughing croaks that begins with a short, gruff note and falls into a series of *kheeyaahhh* sounds. This opportunistic feeder will scavenge for seeds, grains, grasses, fish, fruit, dead fish, and marine invertebrates.

Habitat

Common to Great Lakes coastlines. Breeds on the ground, but may not have a permanent mate, so Ring-billed Gulls often tend to fledglings in pairs or trios.

Local Sites

Common year-round along southern Lower Peninsula shorelines, this gull is often observed in large groups with other species.

FIELD NOTES The Herring Gull, *Larus argentatus* (inset), is our quintessential "seagull." The winter adult plumage of both species look much alike, except the Herring Gull has a red spot on its bill and pink legs.

Breeding | Adult

CASPIAN TERN

Sterna caspia L 21" (53 cm) W 50" (127 cm)

FIELD MARKS

Large, thick, coral red bill

Pale gray with white underparts

Black cap extends from bill to nape and drops below eye

In flight, shows dark underside of primaries and slightly forked tail

Behavior

Often hovers before plunge-diving for small fish, its principle food source. Also sits gull-like and feeds from the water's surface. This largest tern is quite predatory in nature, frequently stealing catches from other gulls and terns, and feeding on their eggs and chicks. Adult's calls include a harsh *kowk* and *ca-arr*. Juvenile call is high, thin whistle *whee-you*.

Habitat

Small colonies nest together on coastlines or in wetlands.

Local Sites

Most common in summer along shorelines in northern Michigan, Caspian Terns are probably best observed around Saginaw Bay and western Lake Erie.

FIELD NOTES Compare the larger Caspian Tern to the smaller Common Tern, *Sterna hirundo* (inset). Note the Common's smaller head and bill. In flight, the Common Tern's tail is noticeably more deeply forked, and the underwing tips are more white, with a thin black line extending from the tip to midwing.

Breeding | Adult

FORSTER'S TERN

Sterna forsteri L 14½" (37 cm) W 31" (79 cm)

FIELD MARKS
Black cap and nape on breeding adult

Orange-red bill with dark tip

Pale gray upperparts

Snow-white underparts

Orange legs and feet

Behavior

When feeding, the Forster's flies back and forth over the water. May forage on insects, picking them from the water's surface. Also plunge-dives to capture small fish. Often gives a one-note call while feeding over water, or during breeding season: a hoarse *kyarr*.

Habitat

Prefers coastal areas, but also inhabits inland marshes and lakes with abundant fish and insect populations.

Local Sites

Look for the Forster's Tern in the summer breeding season around Saginaw Bay and coastal marshlands of the southeastern Lower Peninsula.

FIELD NOTES The Forster's Tern and the Black Tern, *Chlidonias niger* (inset), breed near each other in marshes. At times, the young of each species may wander into the territory of the other species. Note the darker gray upperparts and gray-black cap behind the eyes of the juvenile Black Tern versus the black eye patch and patchy brown upperparts on the juvenile Forster's Tern. In non-breeding plumage, both species are whiter but note the black head patch and darker legs of the Black Tern to distinguish the two species.

Year-round | Adult

ROCK PIGEON

Columba livia L 12½" (32 cm)

FIELD MARKS
Highly variable, multicolored

Head and neck usually darker than back

White rump

Dark band at end of tail

Black bars on inner wing

Behavior

Feeds during the day on grain, seeds, fruit, or refuse in parks and fields. Frequently visits backyard feeding stations. As pigeons forage, they move with a short-stepped, stodgy gait—"pigeon-toed"—while their heads bob fore and aft. Characterized by soft *coo-cuk-cuk-cuk-cooo* call. In courtship display, male turns in circles while cooing. Courtship can result in a pairing for life. Nest is built of stiff twigs, sticks, leaves, and grasses.

Habitat

Widespread throughout United States in many areas, especially urban environments. Makes a flimsy nest on ledges or rooftops, which may be reused or built over in subsequent years, and made more sturdy by the hardened feces left by their broods.

Local Sites

Introduced from Europe by early settlers, this pigeon is now widespread and common. Easily observed in urban parks and fields.

FIELD NOTES The colors of the Rock Pigeon's plumage, ranging from rust red to multicolored, developed over centuries of near domestication. Those resembling their wild ancestors have head and neck darker than back, two black wing bars, a white rump, and a black band at end of tail.

Year-round | Adult

MOURNING DOVE

Zenaida macroura L 12" (31 cm)

FIELD MARKS

Small, buffy head with black spot on lower cheek; pinkish wash on neck

Trim-bodied, with long tail tapering to a point

Brownish gray upperparts, black spots on upper wings

Behavior

Generally a ground feeder, a Mourning Dove will forage for grains and other seeds, grasses, and insects. Known for its mournful call, *oowooo-woo-woo-woo*, sometimes repeated several times. Wings produce a fluttering whistle as the bird takes flight. A very successful breeder, a Mourning Dove may have several broods during a breeding season, each one consisting of two or three chicks.

Habitat

Found in a variety of habitats, the Mourning Dove prefers an open setting, often choosing urban or suburban sites for feeding and nesting, including front porch eaves.

Local Sites

This is the most abundant and widespread dove. It's most easily discovered in habitats having both trees and open ground.

FIELD NOTES A Mourning Dove pair make very attentive parents, and it is rare for them to leave eggs unattended. The male will usually incubate the eggs from midmorning until late afternoon while the female forages, and the female will tend the nest the rest of the day. Clutches consist of two eggs, but a pair may hatch up to six clutches in a year.

Year-round | Adult

YELLOW-BILLED CUCKOO

Coccyzus americanus L 12" (31 cm)

FIELD MARKS

Grayish brown above, white below

Rufous primaries

Yellow lower mandible

Undertail patterned in bold black and white

Behavior

Unique song sounds hollow and wooden, a rapid staccato *kuk-kuk-kuk* that usually descends to a *kakakowlp-kowlp* ending. This shy species slips quietly through overgrowth, combing vegetation for caterpillars, frogs, or insects. During courtship, male will climb on female's shoulders to feed her from above.

Habitat

Common in the dense canopies of woods, orchards, and streamside willow and alder groves throughout eastern and midwestern U.S. Also inhabits tangles and vines of marsh and swamp edges. Nests lined with grasses and moss found on horizontal tree limbs.

Local Sites

More often heard than seen, the best chances of observing a Yellow-billed is during the summer in woods like Port Huron State Game Area or Bald Mountain State Recreation Area.

FIELD NOTES Sharing not only habitat, but nests too, the Black-billed Cuckoo, *Coccyzus erythropthalmus* (inset), is known to sometimes lay its eggs in the nests of Yellow-billeds. It is best distinguished by a dark bill, red eye ring, and less bold spots on the underside of the tail.

Year-round

GREAT HORNED OWL

Bubo virginianus L 22" (56 cm)

FIELD MARKS
Large overall size

Long ear tufts (or "horns")

Rusty facial disks

Yellow eyes

White chin and throat

Behavior
Chiefly nocturnal, feeds on a wide variety of animals including skunks, porcupines, birds, snakes, grouse, and frogs. Watches from high perch, then swoops down on prey. Call a series of three to eight loud, deep hoots, the second and third hoots often short and rapid.

Habitat
The most widespread owl in North America, the Great Horned Owl can be found in a wide variety of habitats, including forests, cities, and wood lots.

Local Sites
Look for the Great Horned in the Sault Ste. Marie or Whitefish Point areas. An easily observed Great Horned Owl nest can be seen at Metro Beach Metropark.

FIELD NOTES Slightly larger than the Great Horned Owl, the Snowy Owl, *Bubo scandiacus* (inset), visits Michigan in the winter months. Note the female Snowy may retain more of the dark brown markings found on the immature throughout her life. Males, as they age, may become almost entirely white.

Year-round | Adult

BARRED OWL

Strix varia L 21" (53 cm)

FIELD MARKS
Large, chunky owl with dark eyes, darkly-ringed facial disk

Brown overall, with dark barring on upper breast and streaking below

Lacks ear tufts

Wings appear rounded in flight

Behavior
Pursues small mammals such as mice, squirrels, and rabbits by watching from perch, or by flying low over ground, sometimes hovering before dropping down to clutch prey in its talons. Nests in tree hollows. Call is a distinctive *who-cooks-for-you, who-cooks-for-you-all* or a drawn-out *hoo-ah.*

Habitat
Dense woodlands, mixed woods of rivers or swamps. Often sharing territory with the Great Horned, the Barred is much less aggressive and will steer clear of a Great Horned in its territory.

Local Sites
The Barred Owl is resident in the entire state of Michigan, though less common in the Lower Peninsula. It is sometimes heard or spotted during the daytime. Look carefully in Warren Woods State Park.

FIELD NOTES Recent studies of nesting Barred Owls, using cameras and microphones in nest boxes, have shown that Barred Owls routinely use up to ten different calls, each for a specific purpose. Owls usually show little variation of the geographic dialect often seen in other species of birds, but the calls of males do differ from females.

Year-round | Red morph

EASTERN SCREECH-OWL

Megascops asio L 8½" (22 cm)

FIELD MARKS
Small, with yellow, immobile eyes
and pale bill tip

Underparts marked by vertical
streaks crossed by dark bars

Ear tufts prominent if raised

Round, flattened facial disk

Behavior
Nocturnal owl; uses heightened vision and hearing to
hunt for mice, voles, shrews, and insects. If approached
while roosting during the day, it will elongate its body,
erect its ear tufts, and close its eyes to blend into its
background. Red and gray morphs occur in Michigan.
Emits a series of quavering whistles, descending in
pitch, or a long, one-pitch trill. This trill in particular is
used by a pair or family to contact one another.

Habitat
Common in a wide variety of habitats including woodlots, forests, swamps, orchards, parks, and suburban
gardens. Nests in trees about 10 to 30 feet up. Also
known to use man-made nesting boxes.

Local Sites
Generally prefers woodland, look for signs of the
Eastern Screech-Owl in Shiawassee National
Wildlife Refuge—and in your own backyard. Its call
is rather easy to imitate and owls respond readily.

FIELD NOTES The Eastern Screech-Owl is known to eat a variety
of songbirds. During daylight hours, listen for flocks of small
songbirds mobbing an owl. They are more likely to find an owl
than you are.

Year-round | Adult

COMMON NIGHTHAWK

Chordeiles minor L 9½" (24 cm)

FIELD MARKS

Long, pointed wings with pale spotting; tail slightly forked

Bold white bar across primaries, bar on tail in males only; dark, mottled back

Underparts whitish with bold dusky bars, darker in males

Behavior

The Common Nighthawk's streamlined body allows agile aerial displays when feeding at dusk. Hunts in flight, snaring insects. Drops lower jaw to create opening wide enough to scoop up large moths. Roosts on the ground, scraping a shallow depression, or on branches, posts, or roofs. Call is a nasal *peent*. Throat is white in the male, pale buff in females. Male's wings make hollow booming sound during courtship display.

Habitat

Frequents woodlands and shrubby areas; also seen in urban and suburban settings.

Local Sites

May often be seen feeding near bright city lights to which insects are drawn. Usually sighted in Michigan during the late summer or early fall; look for it chasing insects above rooftops, or at dusk in Seney National Wildlife Refuge.

FIELD NOTES Another nighttime insect hunter, the Whip-poor-will, *Caprimulgus vociferus* (inset), hunts on the wing for moths and mosquitoes and sleeps on the ground during the day. It in most easily identified in the field by its loud, clear, and mellow song: *whip-poor-will*.

Year-round | Adult

CHIMNEY SWIFT

Chaetura pelagica L 5¼" (13 cm)

FIELD MARKS
Cigar-shaped body

Short, stubby tail

Dark plumage, sooty gray overall

Long, narrow, curved wings

Blackish gray bill, legs, feet

Behavior
The Chimney Swift flies with long wings at great speeds, often in a circle. Catches ants, termites, and spiders while in flight. Groups of Chimney Swifts may circle above a chimney at dusk before dropping in to roost. Makes a high-pitched chattering call. During aerial courtship, a pair flies with their wings held in a "V" above their backs, rocking from side to side.

Habitat
Builds cup-shaped nests of small twigs and saliva in chimneys, under eaves of abandoned barns, and in hollow trees. Roosts in chimneys and steeples. Otherwise seen soaring over forested, open, or urban sites.

Local Sites
In the summer, look for Chimney Swifts soaring above urban and suburban settings, foraging for flying insects

---

FIELD NOTES Before the European settlement of North America, the Chimney Swift nested in hollow trees. It has since adapted to artificial nesting sites, such as chimneys, air shafts, vertical pipes, barns, and silos. It is the only swift in the eastern U.S. and southeastern Canada. It winters in the Amazon Basin.

Year-round | Adult male

RUBY-THROATED HUMMINGBIRD

Archilochus colubris L 3¼ (8½ cm)

FIELD MARKS
Metallic green above

Adult male has brilliant red throat, black chin, whitish underparts, dusky green sides

Female has whitish throat, grayish white underparts, buffy wash on sides

Behavior
The Ruby-throated Hummingbird probes backyard hummingbird feeders and flowers for nectar while hovering virtually still in midair. Also feeds on small spiders and insects. When nectar is in short supply, it is known to drink sap from wells made in tree trunks in early spring by sapsuckers. In spring the male Ruby-throateds arrive on breeding grounds before the females and engage in jousts to claim prime territory. Once mated, females build nests on small tree limbs and raise young by themselves.

Habitat
Found in gardens and woodland edges throughout most of eastern United States.

Local Sites
Abundant through the summer in backyard flower gardens and at hummingbird feeders.

FIELD NOTES Hummingbirds and the flowers they pollinate have both adapted to meet each other's needs. Typical flowers favored by the hummingbird are narrow and tubular, the nectar accessible only to a long bill or tongue. Hummingbirds are attracted to bright red, orange, and pink, and flowers' subtle color patterns may signal nectar availability to the birds.

Year-round | Male

BELTED KINGFISHER

Ceryle alcyon L 13" (33 cm)

FIELD MARKS

Blue-gray head with large, shaggy crest; blue-gray upperparts and breast band

Long, heavy black bill; white collar, underparts.

Female has rust flanks and belly band

Behavior

Generally solitary and vocal, dives for fish from a waterside perch or after hovering above in order to line up on its target. Will also feed on insects, amphibians, and small reptiles. Call is a loud, dry rattle, often given when alarmed, to announce territory, or while in flight. The Belted Kingfisher is one of the few species in North America in which the female is more colorful than the male, which lacks the female's rust belly band and flanks.

Habitat

Common and conspicuous along rivers, ponds, lakes, and coasts. Prefers areas that are partially wooded.

Local Sites

Kingfishers can be found on waterways around Saginaw Bay or in Maple River State Game Area.

FIELD NOTES Belted Kingfisher pairs are monogamous and nest in tunnels which they excavate in vertical, earthen banks near clear water. Both sexes build the nest and share parenting duties for their clutches of three to eight. Mated pairs renew their relationship with each breeding season, engaging in courtship rituals such as dramatic display flights, the feeding of the female by the male, and vocalizations.

Year-round | Adult male

RED-BELLIED WOODPECKER

Melanerpes carolinus L 9¼" (24 cm)

FIELD MARKS
Black and white barred back

White uppertail coverts

Central tail feathers barred

Red nape; red crown only
on males

Reddish tinge on belly

Behavior
Climbs tree trunks by bracing itself with stiff tail,
taking strain off short legs. Chisel-shaped bill drills in
and through tree bark to extract grubs, worms, fruits,
and seeds. Also known to feed on sap from wells made
by sapsuckers, and on sunflower seeds and peanut
butter in feeders. Call is a rolling *churr* or *chiv-chiv* that
rises and falls, reminiscent of the whirring of wings.

Habitat
Common in open woodlands, forest edges, suburbs,
and parks. Nests and roosts at night in tree cavities.

Local Sites
Although primarily a southern species, the Red-bellied
Woodpecker has adapted to life farther north,
especially in Warren Woods State Park.

FIELD NOTES The related Red-headed Woodpecker,
Melanerpes erythrocephalus (inset), is similar in size
to the Red-bellied, but has an entirely red head,
neck, and throat that contrasts with a blue-black
back and snow-white underbelly. The Red-headed
utters a loud *queark* similar to the Red-bellied, but
harsher and sharper in tone.

Year-round | Female "Yellow-shafted"

NORTHERN FLICKER

Colaptes auratus L 12½" (32 cm)

FIELD MARKS
Brown, barred back; white rump;
cream underparts with black
spotting; and black crescent bib

Gray crown, tan face with red
crescent on nape; and, on male,
black moustachial stripe

Behavior
Feeds mostly on the ground, frequently on ants—
digging into the dirt and lapping them up with its long,
barbed tongue. Known to consume poison ivy berries.
A cavity-nesting bird, the Northern Flicker will drill
into wooden surfaces above ground, including utility
poles and houses. Call is a long, loud series of *wick-er,
wick-er* on breeding grounds, or a single, loud *klee-yer*
year-round.

Habitat
Prefers open woodlands and suburban areas with
sizeable living and dead trees. As insectivores, Northern
Flickers are at least partially migratory, moving southward in the winter in pursuit of food.

Local Sites
Look for it perched near its nest on a tree in wooded
parks like those in Maple River State Game Area.

FIELD NOTES Once considered separate species, two distinct
groups make up the Northern Flicker species. The "Red-shafted
Flicker" is most often seen in the western U.S. The "Yellow-
shafted Flicker," described above, is the subspecies commonly
seen in the eastern and northern United States.

Year-round | Adult male

YELLOW-BELLIED SAPSUCKER

Sphyrapicus varius L 8½" (22 cm)

FIELD MARKS
Red forecrown on black and white head

Chin and throat red in male, white in female

Blackish back with white rump

Yellowish underparts

Behavior
Drills evenly spaced rows of holes in trees, then visits these "wells" for sap and the insects they attract. Also pecks insects from trunks in more typical woodpecker fashion, and will sometimes fetch them from the air. Also eats berries and fruit, depending on season and availability of preferred foods. Call is a nasal *me-ah*.

Habitat
Woodlands, aspen groves, and orchards. Makes its nest in cavities of trees, often using the same tree for nesting in consecutive years, but rarely the same nest hole.

Local Sites
During summer breeding season, look for the Yellow-bellied Sapsucker's characteristic holes in tree trunks in areas such as Manistee National Forest, or in other wooded parklands in the northern half of the state.

FIELD NOTES The Yellow-bellied Sapsucker is the only species of woodpecker in the eastern U.S. that is fully migratory. It makes two kinds of holes in trees: a rounded hole that extends deep within the tree and is not enlarged, and a shallower, rectangular hole that must be continually maintained to keep sap flowing.

Year-round | Adult male

DOWNY WOODPECKER

Picoides pubescens L 6¾" (17 cm)

FIELD MARKS
White belly, back, outer tail feathers; black wings with white spots

Black, stubby bill

Black malar stripe, black cap and ear patch; red occipital patch on male only

Behavior
Smallest woodpecker in North America; forages mainly for insects, larvae, and insect eggs. Will also eat seeds and readily visits backyard feeders for sunflower seeds and suet. Call is a high-pitched but soft *pik*. Note the dull spots or bars on the white outer tail feathers.

Habitat
Common in suburbs, parks, and orchards as well as in forests and woodlands.

Local Sites
A Michigan resident, look for this little woodpecker clinging to trees and foraging in areas such as Proud Lake State Recreation Area near Pontiac.

FIELD NOTES The larger Hairy Woodpecker, *Picoides villosus* (inset), is similarly marked but its bill is as long as its head, and its white outer tail feathers are unmarked. Hairy and Downy Woodpeckers may share the same territory, but the Downy forages on smaller branches, while the Hairy tends to spend more time on the trunk.

Year-round | Male

PILEATED WOODPECKER

Dryocopus pileatus L 16½" (42 cm)

FIELD MARKS
Red cap and crest

Gray bill; male has red
submoustachial stripe

Black overall with white stripe
running from cheek down side

White wing linings

Behavior
The largest woodpecker in North America—except for
the Ivory-billed, which is presumably extinct—the
Pileated Woodpecker is about the size of a crow; and its
deep, slow wing beats mimic a crow's flight. Though
both sexes are alike, the red cap is less extensive in the
female, and the female is less aggressive in producing
the loud, resonant, territorial drumming. Call is a loud
wuck note or series of notes, given in flight.

Habitat
The Pileated Woodpecker is fond of carpenter ants, so
it prefers dense, mature woods where it can seek out
the ants by making long, rectangular or oval holes in
the trunks or stumps of fallen trees.

Local Sites
Found year-round throughout most of Michigan, the
Pileated Woodpecker is known to reside in Hartwick
Pines State Park.

FIELD NOTES The ant-finding excavations of the Pileated Woodpecker are so extensive and deep that they may fell small trees.
These holes also tend to attract other species of birds, such as
wrens and other woodpeckers. A juvenile Pileated Woodpecker
has similar plumage to the adult but it is duller and tends to be
more brownish in color.

Year-round | Adult

EASTERN WOOD-PEWEE

Contopus virens L 6¼" (16 cm)

FIELD MARKS

Dark grayish above and on breast

Dull white throat

Underparts whitish or pale yellow

Adult bill has black upper
mandible, orange lower mandible

Behavior

The Eastern Wood-Pewee generally remains perched
while hunting, with little movement of its wings or
tail; it can be difficult to spot in the canopy. Listen
for its distinctive song: a clear, slow, plaintive *pee-a-
wee,* the second note lower, often alternating with a
downslurred *pee-yer.* Calls include a loud *chip* and clear
whistled, rising *pwee.* When it sights prey, such as flies,
spiders, butterflies, or ants, the bird will fly out to
snatch it, then often return to the same perch.

Habitat

Common in a variety of woodland habitats, favoring
open areas over densely packed forests.

Local Sites

Visit Manistee National Forest during the summer
to encounter the Eastern Wood-Pewee.

FIELD NOTES Population studies over the last 25 years suggest
that the Eastern Wood-Pewee's numbers are in decline—in part,
because of the species' low reproduction rate. At the same time,
exploding populations of white-tailed deer are overbrowsing
woodlands, damaging the intermediate canopy upon which the
birds depend. Finally, suitable nesting areas of the Wood-pewee
are being further eroded by fire-fighting efforts to keep forests
clear of dead trees and underbrush.

Nonbreeding | Adult

EASTERN PHOEBE

Sayornis phoebe L 7" (18 cm)

FIELD MARKS
Brownish gray above, darkest on head, wings, and tail

Underparts mostly white with pale olive wash on sides and breast

Fresh fall birds are washed with yellow below

Behavior
The Eastern Phoebe is distinguished from the Eastern Wood Pewee (see p. 137) by its habit of pumping its tail up and down and spreading it while perched. The phoebe waits for prey to pass, and then flies out to capture it, often returning to its previous perch. Its distinctive song, a buzzy *fee-bee,* is accented on the first syllable, and its call note is a sharp *chip.*

Habitat
Found in a variety of habitats, including woodlands, farmlands, and suburbia. The Eastern Phoebe is known to nest under bridges, in eaves, or in rafters. Its nest is constructed with mud and moss, and may be lined with feathers or hair.

Local Sites
Common to the entire state of Michigan in the summer, look for the Eastern Phoebe in its natural breeding habitat in Rifle River Recreation Area.

FIELD NOTES The Eastern Phoebe was the first bird to be banded in North America. In 1804, John James Audubon attached silver thread to the leg of this species to track its return in successive years.

Juvenile

EASTERN KINGBIRD

Tyrannus tyrannus 8½" (22 cm)

FIELD MARKS
Black head

Slate gray back

Tail has broad white terminal band

White underparts

Pale gray wash across breast

Behavior
Waits on perch until it sees an insect, then catches prey in midair and returns to perch to eat. Raspy call when feeding or defending, sounds like *zeer;* also uses a harsh *dzeet* note alone or in a series. Males court through erratic hovering, swooping, and circling, revealing otherwise hidden crown patch.

Habitat
Common and conspicuous in woodland clearings or open fields with small forest stands, farms, and orchards. Builds cup-shaped nest of weeds, moss, and feathers near the end of a horizontal tree branch, sometimes on a post or stump.

Local Sites
The varied habitats at Good Harbor Bay provide for a variety of birds. The Eastern Kingbird visits here during summer months.

FIELD NOTES The Eastern Kingbird has a red crown patch that is rarely seen unless the bird feels threatened or is displaying, raising the feathers on its head into a crest. Living up to its Latin name, which means "tyrant of tyrants," the Eastern Kingbird will actively defend its nest, sometimes pecking at and even pulling feathers from the backs of hawks, crows, and vultures.

Year-round | Adult

YELLOW-THROATED VIREO

Vireo flavifrons L 5½" (14 cm)

FIELD MARKS
Bright yellow spectacles, throat, and breast

White belly, two white wing bars

Upperparts olive, contrasting gray rump

Behavior
Vireos eat a variety of food in several manners, from snatching insects in aerial foraging, to eating berries in anticipation of migration. Its song is a slow repetition of buzzy two or three note phrases, often containing a rising *three-eight*.

Habitat
Usually a bird of open deciduous forests, thriving best in areas covering more than 250 acres.

Local Sites
June is a good time to hear and see Yellow-throated Vireos foraging for their broods in Stinchfield Woods around Ann Arbor.

FIELD NOTES Compare the Yellow-throated Vireo with the related White-eyed Vireo, *Vireo griseus* (inset), which is more gray than olive above, with pale yellow sides and flanks, and also has yellow spectacles. Note, however, the White-eyed Vireo's distinctive white iris, visible at close range. It prefers a shrubby habitat, and is very rare as far north as Michigan.

Year-round | Adult

RED-EYED VIREO

Vireo olivaceus L 6" (15 cm)

FIELD MARKS
Blue-gray crown

White eyebrow, bordered above
and below in black

Olive back, darker wings and tail

White underparts

Ruby red eye, visible at close range

Behavior
Searches through foliage for fruits, berries, and
especially caterpillars. Sometimes hovers to snatch
food from high branch. Song a variable series of
deliberate, short phrases, sung nearly without end from
dawn through dusk and while brooding, foraging,
roosting, and even swallowing. Male known to chase
femaleduring courtship, sometimes even pinning her
to the ground.

Habitat
Common in the forest canopies of eastern deciduous
woodlands. Builds nests of grass and forest debris on
horizontal tree limbs.

Local Sites
Look, but especially listen, for the Red-eyed Vireo in
Bald Mountain State Recreation Area during the
summer months.

FIELD NOTES The Red-eyed Vireo is one of the most common
songbirds in North America. Its sing-song *here-I-am, where-are-
you* voice is easily recognized during the hot summer months.
The otherwise secretive vireo prefers caterpillars and other
insects to eat during breeding season. It is often theunwitting
host for the Brown-headed Cowbird, which lays its eggs in the
vireo's nest.

Year-round

BLUE JAY

Cyanocitta cristata L 11" (28 cm)

FIELD MARKS
Dull blue crest and back

Black barring and white patches
on blue wings and tail

Black necklace on whitish
underparts

Bristles cover nostrils

Behavior

Noisy, bold Blue Jays are noted for their loud, piercing
call of *jay-jay-jay* when alarmed, their musical *weedle-
eedle*, and their imitations of several hawk species. A
two-note vocalization and a bobbing display may be
observed during courting. Often seen in small family
groups, foraging for insects, nuts, and berries. Blue Jays
are also known to raid nests for eggs and nestlings of
other species.

Habitat

Once primarily a deciduous forest dweller, the Blue
Jay has adapted to fragmented woodlands, parks,
suburban backyards, even cities. Builds nests of twigs,
bark, moss, and discarded paper or string in oak and
beech trees 5 to 20 feet up.

Local Sites

Blue Jays can be spotted throughout most of Michigan.
If not found in your backyard, try wooded areas like
Seney National Wildlife Refuge.

FIELD NOTES The Gray Jay, *Perisoreus canadensis* (inset), is confined to patches of boreal forest
in the Upper Peninsula. Even bolder than the Blue
Jay, the Gray Jay will steal food from campsites,
or take food offered by hand. It has sooty gray
upperparts, a short bill, and no crest.

Year-round

AMERICAN CROW

Corvus brachyrhynchos L 17½" (45 cm)

FIELD MARKS
Long, heavy, black bill

Black, iridescent plumage overall

Broad wings and short tail

Brown eyes

Readily identified by familiar call

Behavior

Omnivorous. Often forages in flocks, feeding on insects, garbage, grain, mice, eggs, and baby birds. American Crows take turns at sentry duty, perched on guard while a flock feeds; and are regularly seen noisily mobbing larger predators like eagles, hawks, and Great Horned Owls. A crow's bill, while impressive, cannot tear through hide, so it will wait for another predator— or automobile—to open up a carcass for dining. Most readily identified by its familiar call, *caw-caw*.

Habitat

Among the most widely distributed and familiar birds in North America. Lives in a variety of habitats.

Local Sites

Common throughout its range, and readily viewed in the vicinity of landfills and agricultural operations.

FIELD NOTES At 24 inches (61 cm), the Common Raven, *Corvus corax* (inset), is larger than the American Crow, and is readily identified by its guttural croaking call, its wedge-shaped tail, and its larger, heavier bill. In Michigan, the Common Raven is found only in well-wooded northern areas.

Year-round | Adult male

HORNED LARK

Eremophila alpestris L 6¾-7¾" (17-20 cm)

FIELD MARKS

White forehead bordered by black band, which ends in hornlike tufts

Black cheek stripes; dark bill

Pale yellow to white throat and underparts; brown upperparts

Sandy wash on sides and flanks

Behavior

Forages on ground, favoring open agricultural fields with sparse vegetation. Feeds mainly on seeds, grain, and some insects. Seldom alights on trees or bushes. On the ground, the Horned Lark walks rather than hops. Song is a weak twittering; calls include a high *tsee-ee* or *tsee-titi*. Outside breeding season, the birds form large flocks that may number into the hundreds. A Horned Lark will use its bill and feet, equipped with long blunt claws, to scrape shallow depressions where it roosts and nests. Females build the nest and incubate the clutch; both sexes feed the young.

Habitat

Prefers dirt fields, gravel ridges, and shores.

Local Sites

Making its year-round home in the southern half of the Lower Peninsula, the Horned Lark breeds in the extensive agricultural areas found there.

FIELD NOTES The male engages in a spectacular display flight, ascending several hundred feet into the air while singing, then plummeting headfirst toward the ground, flaring wings at the last second. It is the only true lark native to North America.

Breeding | Adult male

TREE SWALLOW

Tachycineta bicolor L 5¾" (15 cm)

FIELD MARKS

Dark, glossy greenish blue above, white below

Juveniles gray-brown above

White cheek patch; does not extend above eye

Slightly notched tail

Behavior
Often seen in huge flocks during migration. Forages for insects in flight, but may change to a diet of berries or plant buds during colder months, when insects are less abundant. Its song consists of a series of twitters and whistles.

Habitat
Common in wooded habitats near water or where dead trees provide nest holes. Also favors nesting in man-made nest boxes. It lines the nest with feathers, often from other species of birds, which helps to cut down on parasites like mites as well as keeping the young warm.

Local Sites
Tree Swallows are summer residents throughout Michigan. Look and listen for them at Nayanquing Point State Wildlife Area.

FIELD NOTES Among the world's swallows, the Tree Swallow more regularly feeds on plant material and has a particular fondness for waxy bayberries, for which it has developed a special digesting ability. These adaptations allow it to migrate north sooner than other swallows and linger later in the fall.

Year-round | Adult male

PURPLE MARTIN

Progne subis L 8" (20 cm)

FIELD MARKS
Dark, glossy purplish blue

Female, juvenile gray below

Forked tail

Fluid flight, short glides
alternating with rapid flapping

Behavior
The Purple Martin forages almost exclusively in flight,
darting for wasps, bees, dragonflies, winged ants, and
other insects. Long, sharply pointed wings and a
substantial tail allow it graceful maneuverability in the
air; but feet and legs are small, so it walks with a weak,
shuffling gait. Capable of drinking, even bathing, in
flight by skimming just over water's surface and
dipping bill, or breast, into water.

Habitat
Common in summer in open habitat where it nests
almost exclusively in man-made multi-dwelling martin
houses. Winters in South America.

Local Sites
Look for flocks of Purple Martins in the summer,
perched in long rows on branches and wires; or visit
the Howard Christensen Nature Center.

FIELD NOTES Eastern Purple Martins are highly dependent on
man-made nesting houses, which can hold many pairs of
breeding adults. The tradition of making martin houses from
hollowed gourds originated with Native Americans, who found
that this sociable bird helped reduce insects around villages
and crops.

Year-round | Adult

BANK SWALLOW

Riparia riparia L 4¾" (12 cm)

FIELD MARKS

Distinct brownish gray breast band, often extending in line down center of breast

Brown upperparts

White throat that curves around rear border of ear patch

Behavior

The smallest swallow, the Bank Swallow nests in large colonies in the banks of rivers, cliffs, gravel pits, or highway cuts. Like other swallows, it is an aerial feeder, pursuing insects in flight. Snaps powerful jaws together to subdue insects that seem too large for it to handle. Flies with shallow, rapid wing beats.

Habitat

Prefers to nest in cavities dug into the earth. The Bank Swallow's colonies may number from ten to several thousand birds.

Local Sites

Colonies of Bank Swallows have been sighted in the St. Ignace area of Mackinac County.

FIELD NOTES The Cliff Swallow, *Petrochelidon pyrrhonota* (inset), has a distinctive, squarish tail and buff-colored rump which distinguish it from all other swallows. Note its dark chestnut and blackish throat, and pale forehead. Makes its nest around bridges, rural settlements, or on cliffs in open country. Nests in colonies, in gourd-shaped mud nest.

Year-round | Adult

BARN SWALLOW

Hirundo rustica L 6¾" (17 cm)

FIELD MARKS
Long, deeply forked tail
Reddish brown throat
Dark blue-black breast band
Iridescent blue upperparts
Cinnamon to buff underparts

Behavior
An exuberant flyer, often seen in small flocks. Catches flying insects in midair as it skims low over a field or pond. Will follow tractors and lawn mowers to feed on the flushed insects.

Habitat
Open farms and fields, especially near water. Has adapted to the presence of people to the extent that it now nests almost exclusively in structures such as barns, bridges, culverts, and garages, in pairs or small colonies. Bowl-shaped nests are made of mud and grass, lined with feathers.

Local Sites
Port Huron State Game Area, and any area with farm buildings and especially bridges that are accessible for nesting, are good spots to observe the Barn Swallow making its acrobatic turns to forage for insects.

FIELD NOTES The juvenile Barn Swallow has pale underparts and a noticeably shorter tail, still with characteristic fork. The world's most widely distributed swallow, it is common and abundant throughout Europe and Asia and winters in southern Africa and South America. An unmated male may kill the nestlings of a mated pair in an attempt to break up the couple and mate with the female.

Year-round

BLACK-CAPPED CHICKADEE

Poecile atricapilla L 5¼" (13 cm)

FIELD MARKS
Black cap and bib

White cheeks

Grayish upperparts

Olive flanks

Greater wing coverts and
secondaries edged in white

Behavior
A popular backyard bird, the Black-capped
Chickadee is often the first to find a new bird feeder.
Its diet may consist mostly of seeds from feeders,
and it will hide food in different locations for later
use. Call is a low, slow, *chick-a-dee-dee-dee*. Song is a
clear, whistled *fee-bee* or *fee-bee-ee*, the first note higher
in pitch.

Habitat
Common in open woodlands, clearings, and suburbs.
Builds its nest of moss and animal fur in cavities in
rotting wood or seeks a man-made nest box.

Local Sites
The Black-capped Chickadee is abundant across the
state, visiting feeders offering sunflower seeds.

FIELD NOTES The slightly larger Boreal
Chickadee, *Poecile hudsonica* (inset), is
found only in the Upper Peninsula, and is
gray-brown above, whitish below, with
white cheeks, black bill, brown sides and
flanks. Fairly common in coniferous forests,
listen for its nasal call: *tseek-a-day-day*.

Year-round | Adult

TUFTED TITMOUSE

Baeolophus bicolor L 6¼" (16 cm)

FIELD MARKS
Gray crest

Distinct blackish forehead

Gray upperparts

Russet wash on sides

Whitish underparts

Behavior
Very active forager in trees, seeking insects; sometimes hangs upside down while feeding. May also be seen holding a nut in its feet and pounding it with its bill. A common visitor to backyard feeders, especially fond of sunflower seeds and suet. Stores surplus feed underground. Male feeds female in courtship. Primary song is a loud, whistled *peter-peter-peter,* but it also employs up to ten groups of calls.

Habitat
Open forests, woodlands, groves, and orchards, as well as urban and suburban parks with large trees and shrubs. Nests in natural cavities, woodpecker holes, man-made boxes, sometimes in fence posts near open pastures surrounded by wooded areas.

Local Sites
Look for the Tufted Titmouse foraging for food on the nature trails of Kensington Metropark.

FIELD NOTES Unintimidated by proximity to humans, the Tufted Titmouse will fly toward people who are making a *pish* sound to attract birds. It is known to swoop down and pluck hair directly from a human's scalp for use in its nest. It may also learn to eat from a human hand.

Year-round

BROWN CREEPER

Certhia americana L 5¼" (13 cm)

FIELD MARKS
Mottled, streaky brown above

White eyebrow stripe

White underparts

Long, thin decurved bill

Reddish brown legs

Behavior
Camouflaged by streaked brown plumage, creepers spiral upward from the base of a tree, then fly to a lower place on another tree in search of insects and larvae in tree bark. A Brown Creeper will also eat fruit and berries when insects are scarce. Its long, decurved bill helps it to dig prey out of tree bark, its stiff tail feathers serving as a prop against the trunk.

Habitat
Prefers forested areas, and builds nests behind loose bark of dead or dying trees. Young begin following their parents not long after fledging.

Local Sites
The Brown Creeper is difficult to spot, so listen for the little insect hunter's call, a soft, vibrant *see,* or its high-pitched variable song of *see-see see-titi-see.* Watch the trunks of trees carefully on Drummond Island in the eastern Upper Peninsula.

FIELD NOTES The Brown Creeper is widespread and generally abundant, but the loss of habitat due to deforestation has affected the population of this small relative of the nuthatch.

Year-round | Adult male

WHITE-BREASTED NUTHATCH

Sitta carolinensis L 5¾" (15 cm)

FIELD MARKS
Black cap

White face and breast

Bluish upperparts; wing and tail feathers tipped in white or black

Rust or brown colored underparts near legs

Behavior

Creeps down tree trunks or branches in search of insects. Will also gather nuts and seeds, jam them into the bark, and hammer or "hatch" the food open with its bill. Song of the White-breasted Nuthatch is typically a rapid series of nasal whistles on one pitch; call is usually a low-pitched, repeated, nasal *yank*.

Habitat

Prefers leafy trees for foraging and nesting; builds a nest with twigs lined with feathers in abandoned woodpecker holes or in natural cavities inside decaying trees.

Local Sites

Look for the agile climber in the trees at West Bloomfield Nature Preserve.

FIELD NOTES The Red-breasted Nuthatch, *Sitta canadensis* (inset), also sports a black cap, but note the black eyeline, white eyebrow, and rust underparts. Its high-pitched, nasal call sounds like a toy tin horn. The Red-breasted prefers fir and spruce forests, foraging on small branches and outer twigs. When it builds its nest, the Red-breasted Nuthatch smears resin on the entrance, perhaps to discourage predators.

Year-round | Adult

HOUSE WREN

Troglodytes aedon L 4¾" (12 cm)

FIELD MARKS
Faint eyebrow

Thin, slightly decurved bill

Grayish brown upperparts

Pale gray underparts

Fine black barring on wings
and tail

Behavior
Noisy, conspicuous, and relatively tame, with a tail often cocked upward. Boldly gleans insects, spiders, and snails from vegetation. While most species of wren forage low to the ground, the House Wren will seek food at a variety of levels, including high in the trees. Sings exuberantly in a cascade of bubbling, whistled notes. Call is a rough *cheh-cheh,* often running together into a chatter.

Habitat
Highly tolerant of human presence, hence common in shrubbery around farms, parks, and urban gardens.

Local Sites
This common visitor to backyard birdhouses is fairly easy to spot or hear in most suburban areas.

FIELD NOTES The Winter Wren, *Troglodytes troglodytes* (inset), has a short, stubby tail, and dark barring on its belly. Its song is a rapid series of melodious trills, and its *kelp-kelp* call is distinct from the House Wren's. The secretive Winter Wren nests in dense brush, especially along stream banks in moist, coniferous woods.

Year-round | Adult

CAROLINA WREN

Thryothorus ludovicianus L 5½" (14 cm)

FIELD MARKS
Deep rusty brown above

Warm buff below

Prominent white eye stripe

White throat

Long, slightly decurved bill

Behavior

Pokes into every nook and cranny on the ground with its decurved bill, looking for insects, spiders, snails, millipedes, fruits, berries, and seeds. May also eat small lizards and tree frogs. From an exposed perch at any time of day or year, the male sings melodious *teakettle-teakettle-teakettle* or *cheery-cheery-cheery,* to which the female often responds with a growl of *t shihrrr.* A pair stays together in its territory throughout the year.

Habitat

Common in concealing underbrush of moist wood-lands and swamps and around human habitation on farms and in wooded suburbs. Nests in any open cavity of suitable size, including old woodpecker holes in trees or stumps, bird boxes, barn rafters, mailboxes, flower-pots, even boots left outside.

Local Sites

The Carolina Wren is a loud and conspicuous bird, easily spotted in Warren Woods State Park.

FIELD NOTES The Carolina Wren is very picky about snow cover. It remains year-round throughout its range except after mild winters with low snowfall, when its range expands northward, or after harsh winters with heavy snowfall, when its range retracts.

Year-round | Adult

MARSH WREN

Cistothorus palustris L 5" (13 cm)

FIELD MARKS

Black cap, bold white eye stripe

Warm brown upperparts with black and white streaking

Rufous sides, flanks, and undertail coverts

Long, slender bill

Behavior

Secretively forages among marsh reeds and grasses for insects, larvae, snails, and, occasionally, other birds' eggs. May be seen alone, with a mate, or in a small colony, depending on the girth and quality of the habitat. Male may sing from exposed perch before heading back under cover of vegetation. Call combines liquid notes with slightly harsh tones and can result in up to 219 different songs. When alarmed by intruder, call is a sharp *tsuk,* often doubled.

Habitat

Common to, but stays hidden in, reedy marshes and cattail swamps.

Local Sites

Like most wrens, the Marsh Wren is often heard before it is seen. Look for it atop tall marsh reeds in swampy areas such as Seney National Wildlife Refuge.

FIELD NOTES The male constructs several spherical nests with side entrances. From them, the female will choose one to finish for incubation. Frequently a male roosts in one of the dummy nests while tending to multiple mates.

Year-round | Adult male

GOLDEN-CROWNED KINGLET

Regulus satrapa L 4" (10 cm)

FIELD MARKS
Orange crown patch on male, bordered in yellow and black; yellow crown patch on female, bordered in black

Olive green upperparts, pale buff underparts

Broad whitish stripe above eye

Behavior
Hovers on rapidly beating wings before dipping down to foliage to eat. Also gleans insects, larvae, and seeds from bark and leaves, reaching into tiny recesses with its short, straight bill. Flits its wings while hopping on branches. Song is almost inaudibly high, consisting of a series of *tsee* notes accelerating into a trill.

Habitat
Common in dense, coniferous woodlands. It is the smallest species able to maintain normal body temperature in subfreezing conditions. Nests fairly high in conifer branches, constructing a spherical nest of lichen, moss, bark, and feathers. Nest is so small that eggs are laid in two layers.

Local Sites
Check the forests in the eastern portions of the Upper Peninsula for the busy Golden-crowned Kinglet.

FIELD NOTES The male Ruby-crowned Kinglet, *Regulus calendula* (inset; male, left), shows red crown feathers when it is agitated. It is further distinguished from the Golden-crowned Kinglet by a white eye ring and darker, duskier underparts.

Breeding | Adult male

BLUE-GRAY GNATCATCHER

Polioptila caerulea L 4½" (11 cm)

FIELD MARKS
Male is blue-gray above, female is grayer

Black line on sides of crown in male's breeding plumage only

Long, black tail with white outer feathers

Behavior
Scours deciduous tree limbs and leaves for small insects or spiders, otherwise sometimes captures prey in flight. May hover briefly. Distinguished by its high-pitched buzz while feeding or breeding. Also emits a querulous *pwee*. Known for scratchy imitations of other birds' songs, a surprise to birders expecting this only from the Mimidae family.

Habitat
Favors woodlands, thickets, and lowland chaparral. Male and female together make cup-like nest of plant fibers, spider webs, moss, and lichen. A disturbance at the nest site early on will cause the couple to depart and rebuild elsewhere.

Local Sites
Look for the Blue-Gray Gnatcatcher in Port Huron State Game Area and Kalamazoo Nature Center.

FIELD NOTES The Blue-gray Gnatcatcher is the northernmost-occurring species of gnatcatcher, and the only one truly migratory. Like some other birds, newly hatched gnatcatchers are altricial—naked and unable to see. Both parents feed the young in the nest for about two weeks, then outside for another three weeks.

Year-round | Adult male

EASTERN BLUEBIRD

Sialia sialis L 7" (18 cm)

FIELD MARKS
Chestnut throat, breast, flanks,
and sides of neck

White belly and undertail coverts

Male uniformly deep blue above

Female grayer blue above

Behavior
Tends to still-hunt from an elevated perch in the open,
dropping to the ground to seize insects and spiders.
The Eastern Bluebird has been observed pouncing on
prey which it has spotted from 130 feet away. Call note
is a musical, rising *chur-lee*, extended in song to *chur-
chur-lee-chur-lee*. In winter may form flocks, and roost
communally in tree cavities or nest boxes at night. During courtship, male will make floating butterfly and
wing-waving displays beside a chosen nesting site.

Habitat
Found in open woodlands, meadows, farmlands, and
orchards. Nests with grass, stems, twigs, and needles in
holes in trees and posts, and in nest boxes.

Local Sites
Check out Howard Christensen Nature Center or the
adjacent Rogue River State Game Area for glimpses of
the Eastern Bluebird from late spring through fall.

FIELD NOTES Serious decline in recent decades is due largely to
competition with the European Starling and the House Sparrow
for nesting sites. The provision of specially designed nesting
boxes by a concerned birding community has resulted in a
promising comeback for the Eastern Bluebird.

Year-round | Adult

WOOD THRUSH

Hylocichla mustelina L 7¾" (20 cm)

FIELD MARKS
Reddish brown above, brightest on crown and nape

Rump and tail brownish olive

White eye ring

White face and chest streaked and spotted

Behavior
The Wood Thrush is one of the most common woodland birds of the East, and is best known for its haunting, loud, liquid song of three- to five-note phrases, each phrase usually ending with a complex trill. Calls include a rapid *pit-pit-pit*. The Wood Thrush has been known to preen itself by rubbing ants on its feathers, perhaps to supplement its own oil.

Habitat
Common in moist deciduous or mixed woods, and seldom seen outside of dense forest. Dependent on this habitat, its numbers have declined dramatically since the mid-1900s. It is also susceptible to being parasitized by Brown-headed Cowbirds.

Local Sites
Port Huron State Game area is an excellent area to look for the elusive Wood Thrush.

FIELD NOTES The Veery, *Catharus fuscescens* (inset), is slightly smaller than the Wood Thrush, but is white below with gray flanks, a grayish face, and an indistinct and incomplete gray eye ring. Its upperparts are reddish brown from crown to tail, and its underparts less spotted. Its song is a descending series of *veer* notes, and its call is a sharp, descending, whistled *veer*, giving rise to its name.

Year-round | Adult female

AMERICAN ROBIN

Turdus migratorius L 10" (25 cm)

FIELD MARKS
Gray-brown above with darker
head and tail; white lower belly

Yellow bill

White under chin

Brick red underparts

Behavior
Michigan's state bird, the American Robin is the best
known and largest of the thrushes. Often seen on suburban lawns, hopping about and cocking its head to
one side in search of earthworms. It will also glean
foliage for butterflies, damselflies, and other insects,
and may take such prey in flight. Robins also consume
fruit, usually in the fall and winter. This broad plant
and animal diet makes them one of the most successful
and wide-ranging thrushes.

Habitat
Widespread, seen on grassy lawns. Nests in shrubs,
woodlands, swamps, and parks.

Local Sites
Common throughout its range, backyard birders will
often see this thrush tugging at worms on their
suburban lawns.

FIELD NOTES During the winter, hundreds of robins may gather
together in one roost. Because of this winter gathering, robins
are less abundant elsewhere, although they spend the majority
of the winter in or near their breeding range. In the summer,
females sit on the nest, and males spend the night roosting with
numbers of other males. Female and juvenile robins have paler
breasts than the male, and the juvenile's underparts are tinged
with cinnamon and spotted with brown.

Year-round | Adult

NORTHERN MOCKINGBIRD

Mimus polyglottos L 10" (25 cm)

FIELD MARKS
Gray plumage, dark wings and tail

White wing patches and outer
tail feathers flash conspicuously
during flight

Repeats same phrase several
times while singing

Behavior
This popular mimic is known for its variety of song,
learning as many as 200. Males have a spring and fall
song repertoire. Highly pugnacious, it will protect its
territory against not only other birds but also dogs,
cats, and even humans. Has a varied diet that includes
grasshoppers, spiders, snails, and earthworms.

Habitat
Resides in a variety of habitats, including towns and
suburbs, close to human habitation. Feeds close to the
ground, in thickets or heavy vegetation.

Local Sites
The Northern Mockingbird is a year-round resident of
southernmost Michigan, where it is very rare and local;
only a few pairs breed in the state. To find one, listen
for its characteristic repetition of song phrases three
times before beginning a new one.

FIELD NOTES Sharing the Northern Mockingbird's talent for mimicking the songs of
other birds, the Gray Catbird, *Dumetella
carolinensis* (inset), is most readily identified
by its harsh, descending *mew* call. Plain dark gray
with a black cap and a long, black tail, often cocked. Its undertail
coverts are chestnut.

Year-round

BROWN THRASHER

Toxostoma rufum L 11½" (29 cm)

FIELD MARKS
Reddish brown above

Heavily streaked below

Yellow eyes

Long, reddish brown tail

Immature's eyes may be gray
or brown

Behavior

Forages on or near ground for fruit and grain; finds insects and small amphibians by digging with decurved bill. Song is a long series of varied melodious phrases, each phrase given two or three times. Calls include a *smack* and a *churr*. Courtship involves very little fanfare; the whole process consists of one or both birds picking up some leaves or twigs and dropping them in front of the other.

Habitat

Common in hedgerows, brush, and woodland edges. Often close to human habitation, having adapted to living in the vegetation of the ornamental shrubs of suburban gardens. Nests in bushes, on ground, or in low trees.

Local Sites

The Brown Thrasher is fairly common and widespread. Look for it in brushy areas of Lapeer State Game Area, from spring to fall.

FIELD NOTES A highly creative bird, the Brown Thrasher has the ability to mimic other birds, but more often sings its own song; it's got enough of them. It has been reported that the Brown Thrasher has the largest song repertoire of all North American birds; more than 1,100 types have been recorded.

Nonbreeding | Adult

EUROPEAN STARLING

Sturnus vulgaris L 8½" (22 cm)

FIELD MARKS
Speckled plumage, iridescent
black during breeding

Yellow bill with pink base in
female, blue in male

In fall, darker bill and feathers
tipped in white

Behavior
A highly social and aggressive bird, the European
Starling will gorge on a tremendous variety of food,
ranging from invertebrates—snails, worms, spiders—
to fruits, berries, grains, seeds, and garbage. Will
imitate songs of other species and has call notes that
include squeaks, warbles, chirps, and twittering.

Habitat
Adaptable starlings thrive in a variety of habitats, from
urban centers to agricultural regions. They nest in
cavities ranging from crevices in urban settings to
woodpecker holes and nest boxes.

Local Sites
Widespread, the European Starling is a year-round
resident of the state, and can often be spotted in backyards and most local parks.

FIELD NOTES A Eurasian species introduced to New York in the
1890s that has since spread throughout North America.
Abundant, bold, and aggressive, European Starlings often
compete for and take over nest sites of other birds, including
Eastern Bluebirds, Wood Ducks, Red-bellied Woodpeckers,
Great Crested Flycatchers, and Purple Martins.

Year-round | Adult

CEDAR WAXWING

Bombycilla cedrorum L 7¼" (18 cm)

FIELD MARKS

Distinctive sleek crest

Black mask bordered in white

Silky plumage with brownish chest and upperparts

Yellow terminal tail band

May have red, waxy tips on wings

Behavior

Eats the most fruit of any bird in North America. Up to 84 percent of diet includes cedar, peppertree, and hawthorn berries and crabapple fruit. Also consumes sap, flower petals, and insects. The Cedar Waxwing is gregarious in nature and bands together for foraging and protection. Not strongly territorial, it aggressively defends only its nest, perhaps to guard mate or nesting material. Flocks containing a few to hundreds of birds may feed side by side in winter. Flocks rapidly disperse, startling potential predators.

Habitat

Found in open habitats where berries are available. The abundance and location of berries influence the Cedar Waxwing's migration patterns: It moves long distances only when its food sources run out.

Local Sites

Look for the Cedar Waxwing on berry-ladened branches in Maple River State Game Area

FIELD NOTES The larger, grayer Bohemian Waxwing, *Bombycilla garrulus* (inset), has reddish undertail coverts. An irregular winter visitor to the Upper Peninsula, rarely ranges southward.

Year-round | Adult

PROTHONOTARY WARBLER

Protonotaria citrea L 5½" (14 cm)

FIELD MARKS
Head and underparts golden
yellow, fades to white undertail

Blue-gray wings and tail

Tail has white patches

Female duller

Behavior
The Prothonotary Warbler is the only species of eastern warbler that nests in tree holes rather than in the open, usually selecting a low site along streams or by slow or stagnant water. Song is a series of loud, ringing *zweet* notes, also gives a dry *chip* note and buzzy flight call.

Habitat
Found in damp or swampy wooded areas, searching for insects and larvae on the bark of trees, or by searching on the ground.

Local Sites
A summer resident of southwestern parts of the Lower Peninsula, the Prothonotary Warbler can be found most readily in the Allegan State Game Area.

FIELD NOTES The Prothonotary Warbler has become highly localized in its populations over the years, due to the reduction of its preferred habitat. The term "prothonotory" refers to clerks in the Roman Catholic Church, whose robes were bright yellow.

Year-round | Adult male

GOLDEN-WINGED WARBLER

Vermivora chrysoptera L 4¾" (12 cm)

FIELD MARKS

Black throat and ear patch bordered with white

Yellow crown and wing patch

Blue-gray upperparts; gray-white underparts

Female duller

Behavior

The strikingly marked Golden-winged Warbler regularly hybridizes with the Blue-winged Warbler, which has resulted in declining numbers of the Golden-winged species. Its main song is a soft *bee-bz-bz.*

Habitat

Areas with sparse trees or shrubbery. Abandoned farmland, overgrown pastures, or clear-cut areas are also favored. Nests are built on the ground.

Local Sites

Gratiot-Saginaw State Game Area provides a variety of habitats attractive to the Golden-winged Warbler. Still, declining populations may make this bird a difficult one to see.

FIELD NOTES The Golden-winged Warbler does not remain in one area for very long periods. The more adaptable Blue-winged Warbler tends to displace this warbler where their territories overlap, which adds to the Golden-winged's population decline. It is considered a species of special concern.

Year-round | Adult male

NORTHERN PARULA

Parula americana L 4½" (11 cm)

FIELD MARKS
Gray-blue above with yellowish green upper back; white belly

Two bold white wing bars

Throat and breast bright yellow

Adult male shows reddish and black breast bands

Behavior

A very active forager, the Northern Parula can be observed upside down on tree trunks seeking out larvae; hovering in search of caterpillars or spiders, for which its beak is well adapted; or in aerial pursuit of flying insects. Song can be heard from the treetops during nesting or migration, consisting of a rising, buzz-like trill, which ends with an abrupt *zip*.

Habitat

Common in coniferous or mixed woods, especially near water. Prefers to nest in trees covered with the lichen *Usnea*.

Local Sites

Look in the coniferous areas of the Garden Peninsula for this acrobatic warbler.

FIELD NOTES The distinctive song of the male Northern Parula is easy to recognize—seeing one high in the treetops can be more difficult. Before using your binoculars, search the area where you hear singing until you detect some movement. Then use your binoculars for a better look.

Immature | "Myrtle"

YELLOW-RUMPED WARBLER

Dendroica coronata L 5½" (14 cm)

FIELD MARKS
Bright yellow rump

Yellow patch on sides

Yellow crown patch

White wing bars and tail patches

Females and fall males duller than
breeding males

Behavior
Easy to locate and observe darting about branches
from tree to tree, foraging for insects and spiders in
the spring and summer, for myrtle berries and seeds
in winter. Courtship involves intensive singing. Nest-
building and incubation carried out mainly by the
female. Songs of the eastern subspecies include a slow
warble and a musical trill.

Habitat
Abundant in coniferous or mixed woodlands. Nests
discreetly and solitarily on fork or branch of tree.

Local Sites
Look for the white, black, and yellow underparts of the
Yellow-rumped in the boreal habitats of Hulbert Bog
particularly in spring and early summer.

FIELD NOTES The eastern subspecies of the Yellow-rumped
Warbler is often referred to as "Myrtle Warbler," distinguishing it
from the western subspecies, "Audubon's Warbler," which has
similar markings, but is darker overall with a yellow instead of
white throat and lacks the white eyebrow of the Myrtle. Once
thought to be separate species, this changed when research
showed that they readily hybridize where ranges overlap.

Breeding | Adult male

BLACK-AND-WHITE WARBLER

Mniotilta varia L 5¼" (13 cm)

FIELD MARKS

Boldly striped on head, most of body, and undertail coverts

Male's throat and cheeks are black in breeding plumage; in winter, chin is white

Females and immatures have pale cheeks

Behavior

The only warbler that creeps around branches and up and down tree trunks, foraging like a nuthatch. Probes crevices in the bark of trees with its long bill for insects, caterpillars, and spiders. Song is a long series of high, thin *wee-see* notes; calls include a sharp *chip* and a high *seep-seep*. If disturbed at nest, female drags wings on the ground with tail spread for distraction.

Habitat

Prefers forests, both deciduous and mixed woodlands, as well as forested margins of swamps and rivers. Nests on the ground, close to the base of a bush or tree, or in the hollow of a stump or log.

Local Sites

Often easy to see and identify, the Black-and-white is a resident of Hiawatha National Forest during the summer breeding season.

FIELD NOTES This bird was once referred to as the Black-and-white Creeper because of its creeper- or nuthatch-like feeding behavior. The Black-and-white Warbler returns to its northern breeding grounds about two weeks earlier than most other warblers. It can feed on insects in bark crevices before tree leaves have developed.

Breeding | Adult male

BLACKBURNIAN WARBLER

Dendroica fusca L 5" (13 cm)

FIELD MARKS
Male has fiery orange throat, forehead stripe, triangular black eye
patch and broad white wing patch

Female and fall male paler yellow
throat

Female has two white stripes on
wings, streaked back

Behavior
The Blackburnian Warbler is the only warbler with an
orange throat. It is territorial during the nesting period,
but will associate with other species such as chickadees,
kinglets, and nuthatches after the chicks fledge. The
young will follow the parents while they forage and beg
for food. It will form into small groups only during
migration, and otherwise remains solitary or in its
small family units.

Habitat
Fairly common in coniferous or mixed forests in
northern range, stays mostly in the upper branches.

Local Sites
The eastern sections of Hiawatha National Forest offer
good sighting opportunities for the Blackburnian Warbler during the spring and early summer.

FIELD NOTES The song of the Blackburnian Warbler is a short
series of high notes followed by a squeaky, ascending trill and
ending on a very high note. *zip zip-zip-titititi-tsee*. Because they
tend to remain in the very high branches of trees, they are likely
to be heard before they are seen.

Year-round | Adult female

KIRTLAND'S WARBLER

Dendroica kirtlandii L 5¾" (15 cm)

FIELD MARKS
Blue-gray above with strong black
streaks on back

Yellow below, streaked on sides

Whitish eye ring, broken at front
and rear

Whitish wing bars often indistinct

Behavior

An endangered species, unique to Michigan during
breeding season, the Kirtland's Warbler is one of only a
few warblers known to constantly wag its tail. Its song,
performed primarily by males, is a loud and lively
series of low, sharp notes followed by slurred whistles.

Habitat

An insectivore, this rarest of warblers is only found in
one type of habitat: stands of young jack pines. As a
result, major conservation efforts to preserve the
Kirtland's habitat are underway. The Brown-headed
Cowbird, a nest parasite, is also a threat to this bird.

Local Sites

Known to have active breeding grounds in 12
counties in the Lower Peninsula, and five in the Upper.
The best time to sight the Kirtland's is from mid-May
to early June, and tours are conducted by the U.S. Forest Service out of Mio, and the U.S. Fish and Wildlife
Service from Grayling.

FIELD NOTES The Kirtland's Warbler nests only on the ground or
lowest branches of young jack pines from 5 to 20 feet tall that
are in woodlands 80 acres or more in size. It is estimated that
each mated pair requires as much as ten acres to raise a brood.

Year-round | Adult male

PINE WARBLER

Dendroica pinus L 5½" (14 cm)

FIELD MARKS

Yellow throat color extends onto sides of neck and breast

Male is greenish olive above with dark streaks on sides of breast

Belly and undertail coverts white

Female is duller overall

Behavior
Will feed on ground and along branches for insects, seeds, grapes, and berries, but forages mainly in trees, gleaning insects, caterpillars, and spiders from bark, leaves, and pinecones. Will also dive for flying insects. Visits backyard feeders, especially for suet. Territorially aggressive toward other species sharing the same stand of pines, the Pine Warbler will partition its foraging area into microhabitats according to height within a tree, even inner versus outer branches. A very vocal bird, its song is a twittering musical trill, varying in speed. Call is slurred *tsup*.

Habitat
Favors open stands of pine trees, especially during breeding season. Conceals nest among the needles at tips of pine branches.

Local Sites
A common resident of pine forests. Look in Hartwick Pines State Park for this bright bird.

FIELD NOTES The Pine Warbler is the only warbler to eat large quantities of seed, particularly that from pine trees. Like the Black-and-White Warbler, it arrives earlier in Michigan than most other warblers.

Year-round | Adult male

YELLOW WARBLER

Dendroica petechia L 5" (13 cm)

FIELD MARKS

Bright yellow overall

Plump and short-tailed

Dark eye prominent in yellow face

Male shows distinct reddish streaks below; streaks faint or absent in female

Behavior

Forages in trees, shrubs, and bushes, gleaning insects, larvae, and fruit from their branches and leaves. Will sometimes spot flying insects from a perch and chase them down. Mostly seen by itself or in a pair. Male and female both feed nestlings, sometimes mistakenly giving them noxious, leaf-eating caterpillars. Song is a rapid, variable *sweet-sweet-I'm-so-sweet.*

Habitat

Favors wet habitats, especially those with willows and alders, but also lives in open woodlands, gardens, and orchards. Nests in the forks of trees or bushes at eye level or a little higher.

Local Sites

Damp woodlands and the variety of habitats around Warren Woods State Park offer good sighting locations. Departs Michigan earlier than other warblers in fall; peak migration is late July.

FIELD NOTES A common victim of the cowbird invading its nest, the Yellow Warbler has devised an interesting retaliation tactic. Once foreign eggs are detected, the female will build a new roof of grasses, moss, lichen, and fur over all the eggs, then simply lay a new clutch. A single nest has been found to have up to six stories embedded with cold cowbird and warbler eggs.

Year-round | Adult

OVENBIRD

Seiurus aurocapillus L 6" (15 cm)

FIELD MARK
Russet crown bordered by dark stripes

White eye ring

Olive above

White below with bold streaks and dark spots

Behavior
Generally seen on the ground, walking, rather than hopping, on pinkish legs, with tail cocked. Its song is a loud *teacher-teacher-teacher*, which rises in volume as the song progresses. Sometimes neighboring male Ovenbirds will sing together, one beginning the song, and the second one joining in a few seconds later for several songs.

Habitat
Common on the floor of mature forests, preferring upland or moderately sloped areas. Builds its nest of grasses, twigs, leaves, and pine needles.

Local Sites
Gratiot-Saginaw State Game Area offers a variety of habitats ideal for birding, including hardwood forests favored by Ovenbirds as nesting locations.

FIELD NOTES The Ovenbird gets its name from its covered nest, with its dome shape and side entrance that resembles a Dutch oven. Almost half of all adult Ovenbirds die each year; the oldest known Ovenbird was 11 years old.

Year-round | Adult male

COMMON YELLOWTHROAT

Geothlypis trichas L 5" (13 cm)

FIELD MARKS

Adult male shows broad, black mask bordered above by light gray

Bright yellow throat and breast

Undertail coverts yellow

Female lacks black mask, has whitish eye ring

Behavior

Generally remains close to ground, skulking and hiding itself in undergrowth. May also be seen climbing vertically on stems. While foraging, hops on ground to glean insects, caterpillars, and spiders from foliage, twigs, and grass. Sometimes gleans while hovering or gives chase to flying insects. Song is a loud, rolling *wichity-wichity-wichity-wich*.

Habitat

Predominantly found in wetlands; also low in grassy fields and shrubs. Solitary nester atop piles of weed and grass or in small shrubs. Female builds nest alone from dried grasses and leaves, stems, pieces of bark, and hair.

Local Sites

Hiawatha National Forest's eastern section hosts the Common Yellowthroat between May and August. Keep an eye out also for the Ringed Boghaunter, a rare Michigan dragonfly, during a late May visit to the bogs here.

FIELD NOTES The colors of the Yellowthroat vary widely according to geography. Differences include the amount of yellow on the underparts, the extent of olive shading on the upperparts, and the color of the border between mask and crown, which can go from stark white to gray. The southwestern race, *G. t. chryseola*, is the brightest below and shows the most yellow.

Year-round | Female

AMERICAN REDSTART

Setophaga ruticilla L 5¼" (13 cm)

FIELD MARKS
Male is glossy black overall

Bright orange patches on sides, wings, and tail

White belly and undertail coverts

Female gray-olive above; white below with yellow patches

Behavior
Often fans its tail and spreads its wings when perched, then leaps forth suddenly to hawk flying insects. Also gleans insects, caterpillars, spiders, berries, fruit, and seeds from branches and foliage. Sings often, even in midday heat, in a series of high, thin notes generally followed by a single, wheezy, downslurred note.

Habitat
Common in deciduous and mixed woodlands with viable understory, also in riparian and second-growth woodlands. Nests solitarily in forks of trees or bushes generally 10 to 20 feet from ground in construction combining grasses, bark, roots, lichens, spider webs, and feathers.

Local Sites
The deciduous forest habitats found in Port Huron State Game Area are among the sites favored by the American Redstart for its summer home.

FIELD NOTES An immature male resembles a female. By the first spring, it has gained black lores and some black spotting on the breast, though it still looks more like a female. A year-old American Redstart trying to breed in this plumage is at a great disadvantage, as he has no territory, and it is not until his second fall that he acquires the full adult plumage that will attract a female.

Breeding | Adult male

SCARLET TANAGER

Piranga olivacea L 7" (18 cm)

FIELD MARKS
Breeding male bright red and black

Female has uniformly olive head, back, and rump; darker wings

Fall adult male is yellow-green with black wings

Behavior
The Scarlet Tanager eats fruit and insects. It forages mostly high in the tops of trees, it will also take food from the ground and snag insects on the fly. The male displays to his prospective mate by perching below her, then spreading his wings to show off his scarlet back. The tanager's song is similar to that of the robin, with raspy *querit-queer-query-querit-queer* notes. Call is a hoarse *chip-burr*.

Habitat
Resident of the forest interior, the Scarlet Tanager is often overlooked despite its coloring because of its preference for the forest canopy.

Local Sites
During breeding season, look high in the canopy in Warren Woods State Park or Manistee National Forest for this bright and vocal bird.

FIELD NOTES Recent research suggests that the Scarlet Tanager requires between 25 to 30 contiguous acres of forest to sustain a viable population. In fragmented forests, its nest is vulnerable to predators and to cowbird parasitization. The female Scarlet Tanager sings a similar song to the male's, but hers is softer and shorter. She often sings in response to a male, or while she is gathering nesting materials.

Year-round | Adult female

EASTERN TOWHEE

Pipilo erythrophthalmus L 7½" (19 cm)

FIELD MARKS
Male shows black upperparts

Rufous sides, white underparts

Distinct white patch at base of primaries; distinct white tertials

Females similarly patterned, but black areas replaced by brown

Behavior
Remains low to ground, often scratching it with its feet together, head held low, and tail up. This exposes seeds and insects such as beetles and caterpillars, on which the towhee feeds. Also forages for grasshoppers, spiders, moths, salamanders, and fruit. Known to choose an exposed perch to let out its song of *drink-your-tea*, sometimes shortened to just *drink-tea*. Also calls in a clear, even-pitched, upslurred *swee*.

Habitat
Prefers partial to second-growth woodlands, with dense shrubs, brushy thickets, and extensive leaf litter. Also seen in brambly fields, hedgerows, and forest breaks.

Local Sites
Look for the Eastern Towhee at woodland edges and along the banks of rivers, suh as those found in Maple River State Game Area.

FIELD NOTES The juvenile Eastern Towhee has brown cap, wings, and tail, and is heavily streaked with brown, which is especially distinct on its buff underparts. Look for it only in summer; the molt into full adult colors takes place its first fall.

Nonbreeding | Adult

Spizella arborea L 6¼" (16 cm)

FIELD MARKS

Gray head and nape crowned with rufous; rufous stripe behind eye

Gray throat, breast, with dark spot in center; rufous patches at sides of breast, gray-white underparts

Back streaked with black and rufous; notched tail

Behavior

Despite its name the American Tree Sparrow forages on the ground, nests on the ground, and breeds above the tree line in the far north. Gives a musical *teedle-eet* call, as well as a thin *seet*. Song begins with several clear notes followed by a variable, rapid warble.

Habitat

Although in general this sparrow likes open areas with scattered trees and brush, in the winter it prefers areas near humans, where seeds from bird feeders are plentiful. Eats insects during the breeding season, but eats chiefly seeds and plant matter during the winter.

Local Sites

In winter, watch backyard bird feeders for the American Tree Sparrow, or look for it foraging in shrubby areas throughout the state.

FIELD NOTES The American Tree Sparrow, according to a recent study, apparently prefers looking for predators out of its left eye, possibly because the right hemisphere of the brain processes visual information.

Breeding | Adult

CHIPPING SPARROW

Spizella passerina L 5½" (14 cm)

FIELD MARKS

Breeding adult shows bright chestnut crown

Distinct white eyebrow

Black line extending from bill through eye to ear

Gray nape, cheek, and rump

Behavior

In summer, the Chipping Sparrow forages on the ground for insects. Its nest is usually located within 15 feet of the ground; they are often parasitized by Brown-headed Cowbirds. Song is a one-pitched, rapid-fire trill of dry *chip* notes. Call in flight or when perched is a high, hard *seep* or *tsik*.

Habitat

Very adaptable, the Chipping Sparrow can be found in suburban gardens, city parks, woodlands, orchards, farms, and fields. Rarely nests on the ground, prefer ring branches or vine tangles. One of the tamest of sparrows, it can easily be coaxed into taking food from the hand.

Local Sites

Seney National Wildlife Refuge offers a good location for sighting the Chipping Sparrow.

FIELD NOTES The Chipping Sparrow's winter plumage resembles that of the Field Sparrow, *Spizella pusilla* (inset). Note the Field Sparrow's gray face, reddish crown, pink bill, and pink legs. Song is a clear, plaintive whistle accelerating into a trill. The Field Sparrow prefers open, brushy fields.

Year-round | Adult

SAVANNAH SPARROW

Passerculus sandwichensis L 5½" (14 cm)

FIELD MARKS

Yellow or whitish eyebrow

Pale median crown stripe

Strong postocular stripe

Variable streaked upperparts

Buff to white underparts with variable streaking

Behavior

Forages on the ground for insects, spiders, and sometimes snails in the summer, seeds and berries in the winter. Roosts on the ground in small, close-knit groups. When alarmed, runs through grasses on the ground instead of flying. If pressed, may fly only short distances before dropping back down into grasses. Song begins with two or three *chip* notes, then two buzzy trills. Distinctive flight call is a thin *seep*.

Habitat

Common in a variety of open habitats and grasslands. Can be found on farm fields, meadows, beaches, airports, and grassy dunes. Nests in ground depressions or self-made scrapes in enclaves sheltered by vines or tall grasses.

Local Sites

Most readily found in farmland throughout the state.

FIELD NOTES In many areas of the Savannah Sparrow's range, young birds return to the area where they were born, especially at coastal or island areas. This bird has apparently expanded its range because of human intervention.

Year-round | Adult

SONG SPARROW

Melospiza melodia L 5¾-7½" (16-19 cm)

FIELD MARKS
Upperparts streaked

Underparts whitish, with streaking
on sides and breast

Long, rounded tail

Broad, grayish eyebrow

Broad, dark malar stripe

Behavior
Pumps tail up and down in flight. Scratches ground with
feet to unearth grain, seeds, berries, and insects. Also
forages in trees and bushes and on the ground for larvae,
fruits, and berries. Female broods young while male
defends breeding territory intently, singing from exposed
perches and battling with competitors. Typical song,
though variable, is three to four short, clear notes
followed by a buzzy *tow-wee* and a trill. Distinctive
call is a nasal, hollow *chimp*.

Habitat
Found commonly in suburban and rural gardens,
in weedy fields, and in brushy areas, especially dense
streamside thickets and forest edges. Nests on the
ground or low to it in trees and bushes, hence the
Song Sparrow is one of the most frequent victims of
nest parasitism by the Brown-headed Cowbird.

Local Sites
Rifle River Recreation Area is one of the many
places to find these sparrows in Michigan.

FIELD NOTES Note the darker overall coloring
of the Swamp Sparrow, *Melospiza georgiana*
(inset, breeding plumage). A breeding
adult Swamp Sparrow has a reddish
crown, gray breast, and whitish belly.

Year-round | Adult

WHITE-THROATED SPARROW

Zonotrichia albicollis L 6¾" (17 cm)

FIELD MARKS

Conspicuous and strongly outlined white throat

Dark crown stripes and eye line; yellow in front of eye

Rusty-brown upperparts

Gray-white underparts

Behavior

A frequent visitor to suburban lawns, the White-throated Sparrow sings an ode to Canada, which makes up the majority of its breeding area: *Oh-sweet-Canada-Canada-Canada*. Its calls include a sharp *pink* and a drawn-out, lisping *tseep*.

Habitat

Common in woodland undergrowth, brush, and gardens. Frequents feeders in winter.

Local Sites

Look around Saginaw Bay, especially during migration, for the White-throated Sparrow. During summer months, investigate Seney National Wildlife Refuge.

FIELD NOTES There are two color variations of the White-throated Sparrow: a tan or white eyebrow stripe. Also, the White-throated Sparrow and the Dark-eyed Junco (following page) occasionally mate and produce hybrids. The resulting offspring look like grayish, dully marked White-throated Sparrows with white outer tail feathers.

Year-round | Adult male "Slate-colored"

DARK-EYED JUNCO

Junco hyemalis L 6¼" (16 cm)

FIELD MARKS
Variable dark upperparts, whitish underparts

Gray or brown head and breast, sharply set off in most races

White outer tail feathers in flight

Juveniles of all races are streaked

Behavior
Forages for seeds, grain, berries, insects, caterpillars, and fruit by scratching on ground and gleaning from plants. Will occasionally give chase to a flying insect. Male gathers material for nest, which female builds. Forms flocks in winter, when males may travel farther north than juveniles and females. Song is a musical trill that varies in pitch and tempo. Calls include a sharp *dit,* and a rapid twittering in flight.

Habitat
Breeds in coniferous or mixed woodlands, and in bogs. Winters in a wide variety of habitats throughout much of North America. Nests on or close to ground, either sheltered by a bush, or in a cavity such as a tree root.

Local Sites
Frequenting bird feeders during the winter months, the Dark-eyed Junco is a common sight for most backyard birders. Also visit Seney National Wildlife Refuge during summer months.

FIELD NOTES Once considered five separate species of junco, all five were unified as subspecies of the Dark-eyed Junco by the American Ornithologists' Union in 1973. Although they are widely scattered geographically and highly disparate in their field marks, they do all share white outer tail feathers, their song, their behavioral habits, and, most significant, their genetic makeup.

Breeding | Adult male

SNOW BUNTING

Plectrophenax nivalis L 6¾" (17 cm)

FIELD MARKS

Black-and-white breeding
plumage acquired in spring

Females more brown-and-white
streaked

Bills black in summer, orange-
yellow in winter

Behavior
Calls include a sharp, whistled *tew*, a short buzz, and a
musical rattle or twitter. Song, heard only on breeding
grounds, is a loud, high-pitched musical warbling.
Feeds on seeds and grain in winter.

Habitat
Fairly common, breeding on tundra and rocky shores
or talus slopes. During the winter, is found on rocky
shores, sand dunes, and beaches, and in weedy fields,
grain stubble, or along roadsides in large flocks that
may include Horned Larks.

Local Sites
Look for the Snow Bunting during migration, at the
beaches of Warren Dunes State Park, and in winter in
farm fields throughout the state.

FIELD NOTES Males return to the Arctic breeding grounds first,
followed four to six weeks later by the females. Note the winter
male is lighter in color than the female; she maintains a darker
crown and wings throughout the year. Juveniles are more darkly
streaked brown.

Year-round | Adult male

NORTHERN CARDINAL

Cardinalis cardinalis L 8¾" (22 cm)

FIELD MARKS
Conspicuous crest

Cone-shaped reddish bill

Male is red overall with black face

Female is buffy brown tinged with red on wings, crest, and tail

Juvenile browner; dusky bill

Behavior
Forages on the ground or low in shrubs for a wide variety of insects, but mainly feeds on seeds, leaf buds, berries, and fruit. Readily visits backyard feeders and prefers sunflower seeds. Aggressive in defending its territory, the Northern Cardinal will attack not only other birds, but also itself, reflected in windows, rearview mirrors, chrome surfaces, and hubcaps. Sings a variety of melodious songs year-round, including a *cue cue-cue*, a *cheer-cheer-cheer*, and a *purty-purty-purty*.

Habitat
Year-round resident in suburban gardens, city parks, woodland edges, streamside thickets, and practically any environment that provides thick, brushy cover for feeding and nesting.

Local Sites
Common and abundant around the Lower Peninsula of Michigan year-round, but may be easier to spot in winter months around feeders

FIELD NOTES Another in the family of cardinals, the Rose-breasted Grosbeak, *Pheucticus ludovicianus* (inset: breeding adult male), is slightly smaller than the Northern Cardinal, and sports a similar triangular bill, perfect for cracking seeds. Note the red wing linings.

Breeding | Adult male

INDIGO BUNTING

Passerina cyanea L 5½" (14 cm)

FIELD MARKS
Male breeding plumage
deep blue

Winter male's blue obscured
by brown and buff edges

Female brownish with diffuse
streaking on breast and flanks

Behavior
Related to the grosbeaks and cardinals, the Indigo
Bunting is fairly omnivorous, eating insects, seeds, and
fruit. It prefers insects, however, and will visit feeders
when bugs aren't available. The female builds its cup-
like nest in the branches of trees. Song is a series of
varied phrases, usually paired. Call is a thin, sharp *spit*.

Habitat
Prefers open fields, roadsides, and woodland clearings.

Local Sites
During breeding season, look for the bright blue males
and duller females flitting around Grand River Park.
From a distance or in harsh light, the colorful males
can appear blackish.

FIELD NOTES The Indigo Bunting navigates to and from its breeding and wintering grounds using the stars for guidance. This skill
is believed to be honed when buntings are fledging in the nest.
Because of this skill, experienced adult Indigo Buntings can
return to their previous breeding sites even when they have been
held captive during the winter and released far from their normal
wintering grounds.

Breeding | Adult male

BOBOLINK

Dolichonyx oryzivorus L 7" (18 cm)

FIELD MARKS
Breeding male is entirely black
below; hindneck is buff, fading to
white midsummer; scapulars and
rump white

Female is buffy overall with dark
streaks on head, back, rump and
sides

Behavior
An extraordinary migrant, flying south to the Equator
each autumn. Typically feeds during the day, but
during migration has been observed to feed at night in
agricultural fields such as rice paddies. The male's song
is a loud, bubbling *bob-o-link,* which is often heard in
spring and summer. Flight call, heard year-round, is a
repeated, whistled *ink.*

Habitat
Nests primarily in hayfields or weedy meadows.

Local Sites
Although declining over most of its range because of
loss of habitat or nest destruction from early mowing
of hayfields, the Bobolink is a common sight around
Michigan fields during the summer. Look for it in
Sharonville State Game Area.

FIELD NOTES Male Bobolinks arrive on their Michigan breeding
grounds well before the females. There they stake out territories
and engage in display flights—flying over fields and meadows on
fluttering wings and in full song.

Breeding | Adult male

EASTERN MEADOWLARK

Sturnella magna L 9½" (24 cm)

FIELD MARKS
Pointed bill

Black V-shaped breast
band

Yellow underparts

Outer tail feathers flash white
in flight

Behavior
A strong flier, during which its call is a high, buzzy
drzzt, given in a rapid series. The Eastern Meadowlark
flicks its tail open and shut while foraging on the
ground, feeding mainly on insects during spring and
summer, seeds and agricultural grain in late fall and
winter. Constructs a domed nest on the ground that is
often woven into the surrounding live grasses. Male
known to brood while female starts second nest. Song a
clear *see-you-see-yeeer.*

Habitat
Prefers the open space offered by pastures, prairies,
and farm fields. Common in fields and meadows.
Listen for its rich, musical territorial songs that carry
across the open grasslands it frequents.

Local Sites
Oakwoods Metropark and Indian Springs Metropark
are good spots to look for the Eastern Meadowlark.

FIELD NOTES The Eastern Meadowlark population has been
slowly declining in the eastern states during the past few
decades as its prime habitats are sacrificed to suburban sprawl.
Its breeding range has been advancing northward.

Year-round | Adult male

RED-WINGED BLACKBIRD

Agelaius phoeniceus L 8¾" (22 cm)

FIELD MARKS
Male is glossy black

Bright red shoulder patches
broadly edged with buffy yellow

Females are dark brown above,
heavily streaked below

Behavior
The male Red-winged Blackbird's bright red shoulder
patches are usually visible when it sings from a perch,
often atop a cattail or tall grass stalk, defending its
territory. At other times only the yellow border may be
visible. Territorially aggressive, a male's social status is
dependent on the amount of red he displays on his
shoulders. Runs and hops while foraging for insects,
grass seeds, and agricultural grain in pastures and open
fields. Sometimes considered a threat to crops. Song is a
liquid, gurgling *konk-la-reee,* ending in a trill. Call is a
chack note.

Habitat
Found breeding colonially mainly in freshwater
marshes with thick vegetation. Nests in cattails, bushes,
or dense grass near water. During winter, males and
females flock together and forage in wooded swamps
and farm fields.

Local Sites
Red-winged Blackbirds converge by the thousands in
Erie Marsh Preserve in the fall.

FIELD NOTES Breeding males often have more than one mate and
therefore spend less time caring for young than do the females.
Large flocks are sometimes seen in winter; they may include
other species, such as the Common Grackle.

Year-round | Adult male

COMMON GRACKLE

Quiscalus quiscula L 12½" (32 cm)

FIELD MARKS
Long, keel-shaped tail

Pale yellow eyes

Plumage appears all black; in
good light, males show glossy
purplish blue head, neck, breast

Pointed beak

Behavior
Often nests in small colonies and flocks to large, noisy,
communal roosts in the evening. Mainly seen on the
ground in a group, feeding on insects, spiders, grubs,
and earthworms. Grackles will also wade into shallow
water to forage for minnows and crayfish. Will feast on
eggs and baby birds. Usually mates for life. Courtship
display consists of male puffing out shoulder feathers
to make a collar, drooping his wings, and singing. Birds
produce a sound like a creaky, rusty gate. Call note is a
loud *chuck*.

Habitat
Forages in open spaces provided by farm fields,
pastures, marshes, and suburban yards and gardens.
Requires wooded areas, especially conifers, for nesting
and roosting.

Local Sites
The conifers in Seney National Wildlife Refuge provide
ideal breeding habitat for the Common Grackle.

FIELD NOTES An opportunistic forager, the Common Grackle will
take advantage of whatever food sources it can find. It will follow
plows in fields for exposed invertebrates or mice, wade into
water for fish, or even kill and eat other birds at bird feeders.

Year-round | Adult male

BROWN-HEADED COWBIRD

Molothrus ater L 7½" (19 cm)

FIELD MARKS
Pointed bill

Male's brown head contrasts
with metallic green-black body

Female is gray-brown above,
paler below

Strong, direct flight

Behavior
Cowbirds often forage on the ground among herds
of cattle, feeding on insects flushed by the grazers.
They also feed on grass seeds and agricultural grain.
Generally feed with tails cocked up. Travel and roost in
large flocks after breeding. Song is a squeaky, gurgling
call that includes a squeaky whistle. Brown-headed
Cowbirds are nest parasites and lay their eggs in the
nests of other species, leaving the feeding and fledging
of young to the host birds.

Habitat
Cowbirds prefer the open habitat provided by
farmlands, pastures, prairies and edgelands bordering
woods and forests. Also found in general around
human habitation.

Local Sites
Abundant throughout its range. The Muskegon State
Game Area is a summer home to the cowbird; its
winter occurence in the state is irregular.

FIELD NOTES The Brown-headed Cowbird flourishes throughout
North America. As the cowbird population grows, so does the
number of songbirds—now over 200 species—exposed to its
parasitic brooding habit. The cowbird lays up to 40 eggs a season in the nests of host birds, destroying host eggs and further
depleting endangered species such as the Kirtland's Warbler.

Breeding | Adult male

BALTIMORE ORIOLE

Icterus galbula L 8¼" (22 cm)

FIELD MARKS
Adult male has black hood
and back, orange rump and
underparts

Females are olive-brown above
and orange below, with varying
amounts of black on head

Behavior
The arrival of the brilliantly-colored Baltimore Oriole
is eagerly awaited by birders each spring. Calls include
a rich *hew-li* as well as a series of rattles, and its well-
known melodious song is an irregular series of clear,
whistled notes

Habitat
Common breeder in deciduous woodlands, but also
likes to forage in open areas and tall trees, making it a
common sight in parks and suburbs. Suspends a bag-
shaped nest woven of plant fibers from a branch of a
deciduous tree, usually about 30-feet up—a deterent
to most predators.

Local Sites
The Baltimore Oriole is difficult to miss in its bright
plumage. Look for it in Kensington Metropark.

FIELD NOTES At one time, the Baltimore Oriole and the Bullock's
Oriole were considered the same species, the Northern Oriole.
In fact, although the Baltimore may hybridize with the Bullock's
where their ranges overlap farther west, the two species are not
very closely related. Orioles in North America were so named
after similar birds in Europe. However, orioles here are more
closely related to blackbirds than they are to Old World orioles.

Year-round | Adult male

PURPLE FINCH

Carpodacus purpureus L 6" (15 cm)

FIELD MARKS
Adult male is not purple, but more
rose-red over body and brightest
on head and rump

Females are brown and heavily
streaked below on a whitish belly

Triangular bill with yellowish lower
mandible

Behavior
Visits seed feeders with the look-alike House Finch,
which makes them even more difficult to tell apart. In
some areas, the House Finch has displaced the Purple.
Feeds primarily on seeds, with the seeds from ash trees
making up the bulk of its diet. Song is a rich warbling,
sometimes including songs of other birds. Calls include
a musical *chur-lee* and, in flight, a sharp *pit*.

Habitat
Fairly common in coniferous or mixed woodland
borders, suburbs, parks, and orchards.

Local Sites
Early in the spring or late in the fall, you may see the
Purple Finch migrating through the Saginaw Bay or
Lake Erie Metropark areas.

FIELD NOTES Compare the Purple Finch to the House Finch, *Carpodacus mexicanus* (inset). The head, bib, and rump are typically
red but can vary to orange or yellow. The bib is clearly set
off from streaked underparts, and its tail is squarish.
Female House Finches are generally duller, brown-
streaked overall, and lack distinct eyebrows and
ear patches. Its song is a high-pitched
variation of three-note phrases, including
strident notes, and usually ending with a
nasal *wheer*.

Year-round | Male

RED CROSSBILL

Loxia curvirostra L 6¼" (16 cm)

FIELD MARKS
Bill with crossed tips

Males are reddish overall, brightest
on crown and rump, but may also
be scarlet or yellow

Females are yellow-olive, may show
patches of red, throat is gray

Behavior
The odd crossed tip of the crossbill's bill helps it to get
into tightly closed cones to extract the seeds. It places
its slightly opened bill in between the scales of a cone,
and bites down to pry it open, exposing the seed inside.

Habitat
Fairly common in coniferous woods, the Red Crossbill
may nest at any time of the year, wherever it finds an
abundance of cones, which are the primary food source
for both adults and their young.

Local Sites
The Keweenaw Peninsula makes a year-round home for
the Red Crossbill and the related White-winged Crossbill (below). During the winter months, both crossbills
can usually be found around Sault Ste. Marie and the
Whitefish Point areas.

FIELD NOTES Note the darker black-brown
wings and distinct white wing patches
on the White-winged Crossbill, *Loxia
leucoptera* (inset: male, bottom). The male White-
winged also has a distinct dark bar across his back as
well as a brown-black eye patch, which makes him appear
to be wearing a mask

Breeding | Adult male

AMERICAN GOLDFINCH

Carduelis tristis L 5" (13 cm)

FIELD MARKS
Male bright yellow with black cap;
female duller overall, lacks cap

Black wings have white bars;
male has yellow or greenish
shoulder patch

White uppertail and undertail
coverts

Behavior
The gregarious and active American Goldfinch is often
seen flying overhead as it travels in flocks during the
nonbreeding season. Flocks may contain a hundred or
more birds. Distinctive flight call is *per-chik-o-ree*. The
acrobatic forager hangs upside down to reach seeds or
buds. Visits bird feeders when natural food is scarce.
The finch diet, heavily seeds and vegetable matter, is the
most vegetarian of any North American bird, but it
sometimes eats insects. Song is lively series of trills,
twitters, and *swee* notes.

Habitat
Found in weedy fields, open second-growth woodlands, roadsides. Especially seeks territory rich in
thistles and sunflowers.

Local Sites
Claiming Saginaw Bay as part of its breeding range, the
American Goldfinch is abundant throughout the state
year-round.

FIELD NOTES Sometimes a cowbird will lay its eggs in the nest
of an American Goldfinch. Although the eggs will hatch, most
young cowbirds die before they leave the nest, due to their
inability to obtain enough protein from the finch's seed diet.

Breeding | Adult male

EVENING GROSBEAK

Coccothraustes vespertinus L 8" (20 cm)

FIELD MARKS
Stocky finch with large, pale
yellow or greenish bill

Yellow eyebrow and forehead on
adult male; dark brown and yellow
body, white tertials

Gray-tan female has thin, dark
malar stripe; white-tipped tail

Behavior
Forages mostly in trees and shrubs for seeds and
some berries and insects, sometimes searching on the
ground. Also feeds on buds of deciduous trees, and
some maple sap. At bird feeders, the Evening Grosbeak
is fond of sunflower seeds, and can use its powerful
jaws to crack open seeds easily.

Habitat
Breeds in mixed woods. In winter, frequents woodlots,
shade trees, and feeders. Numbers and range limits
vary greatly. Nest is usually on horizontal branch or
in vertical fork of a tree.

Local Sites
Find this finch at the feeders at Whitefish Point in
spring, and in Eckerman in winter.

FIELD NOTES In flight, take note of the white oval at the base of
the primaries on the underwing of the female Evening Grosbeak,
and the large white patch of white secondaries on the male,
which corresponds to the white patch on the upper wing. The
song of the Evening Grosbeak is a repetition of call notes such
as a ringing trill or *kleeerr,* sometimes similar to a House
Sparrow's song, and a low buzzing *thirr* in flight.

Breeding | Adult male

HOUSE SPARROW

Passer domesticus L 6¼" (16 cm)

FIELD MARKS
Black bill, black bib

Male breeding plumage has
gray crown

Chestnut nape, back, shoulders

Female has streaked back, buffy
eyestripe, unstreaked breast

Behavior

Abundant and aggressive, gregarious in winter. Feeds
on grains, seeds, and shoots, or seeks out bird feeders
for sunflower seeds or millet. Also forages on the
ground, getting food from plants or animal dung. In
urban areas, House Sparrows may beg for food from
humans and will clean up any crumbs left behind.
Singing males give persistent *cheep*. Breeding occurs
in the first year, and pairs mate for life. Females choose
mates mostly according to song display.

Habitat

Found in close proximity to humans. Can be observed
in urban and suburban areas and in rural landscapes
inhabited by humans and livestock.

Local Sites

These nonmigratory birds are common and abundant
year-round throughout Michigan, particularly in the
Lower Peninsula.

FIELD NOTES In courtship, the male stiffly displays for the female
by fanning his cocked tail, sticking out his chest, drooping his
wings slightly, and calling repeatedly as he hops around. Other
males may gather and compete by chasing the female and
singing vigorously.

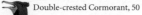

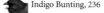

Mostly Brown

 Ruddy Duck, 38

 Ring-necked Pheasant, 40

 Wild Turkey, 42

 Ruffed Grouse, 44

 Pied-billed Grebe, 48

 American Kestrel, 72

 Virginia Rail, 76

 Sora, 78

 American Woodcock, 96

 Great Horned Owl, 112

 House Wren, 168

 Carolina Wren, 184

 Marsh Wren, 172

 Cedar Waxwing, 202

 House Sparrow, 258

Mostly Brown and White

 Canada Goose, 14

 Green-winged Teal, 22

 American Wigeon, 24

 Northern Pintail, 26

 Canvasback, 28

 Osprey, 62

 Bald Eagle, 66

 Red-tailed Hawk, 70

 Semipalmated Plover, 86

 Killdeer, 88

 Greater Yellowlegs, 90

 Spotted Sandpiper, 92

 Upland Sandpiper, 94

 Yellow-billed Cuckoo, 110

 Barred Owl, 114

 Common Nighthawk, 118

 Northern Flicker, 128

 Horned Lark, 150

 Bank Swallow, 156

 Brown Creeper, 164

Mostly Red

 Scarlet Tanager, 216

 Northern Cardinal, 234

 Purple Finch, 250

 Red Crossbill, 252

Mostly White

 Tundra Swan, 12

 Snow Goose, 14

 Great Egret, 52

 Bonaparte's Gull, 98

 Ring-billed Gull, 100

 Caspian Tern, 102

 Forster's Tern, 104

Mostly Yellow

 Yellow-throated Vireo, 142

 Prothonotary Warbler, 192

 Pine Warbler, 206

 Yellow Warbler, 208

 Common Yellowthroat, 212

 Eastern Meadowlark, 240

 American Goldfinch, 254

 Evening Grosbeak, 256

Prominent Green Head

 Wood Duck, 18

 Mallard, 20

 Common Merganser, 36

The main entry for each species is listed in **boldface** type and refers to the text page opposite the illustration.

A check-off box is provided next to each common-name entry so that you can use this index as a checklist of the species you have identified.

ACKNOWLEDGMENTS

The Book Division would like to thank the following people for their guidance and contribution in creating the *National Geographic Field Guide to Birds: Michigan*

Tom Vezo:
Tom Vezo is an award-winning wildlife photographer who is widely published throughout the U.S. and Europe. Located out of Green Valley, Arizona, he specializes in bird photography but photographs other wildlife and nature subjects as well. He is also a contributor to the *National Geographic Reference Atlas to the Birds of North America*. For a look at more of his images, find his gallery at tomvezo.com.

Brian E. Small:
Brian E. Small has been a full-time professional wildlife photographer specializing in birds for more than 15 years. In addition, he has been a regular columnist and Advisory Board member for *WildBird* magazine for the past 10 years. An avid naturalist and enthusiastic birder, Brian is currently the Photo Editor for the American Birding Association's *Birding* magazine. You can find more of his images at www.briansmallphoto.com.

Cortez C. Austin, Jr.:
Cortez Austin is a wildlife photographer who specializes in North American and tropical birds. He has a degree in zoology and has done graduate work in conservation, ecology, and microbiology. An ardent conservationist, he has donated images, given lectures, and written book reviews for conservation organizations. In addition he has published numerous articles and photographs in birding magazines in the United States. His photographs have also appeared in field guides, books, and brochures on wildlife.

Bates Littlehales:
National Geographic photographer for more than 30 years covering myriad subjects around the globe, Bates Littlehales continues to specialize in photographing birds and is an expert in capturing their beauty and ephemeral nature. Bates is co-author of the *National Geographic Photographic Field Guide: Birds,* and a contributor to the *National Geographic Reference Atlas to the Birds of North America*.

Rulon Simmons:
Co-author of the *National Geographic Photographic Field Guide: Birds*, Rulon Simmons worked 32 years for the Eastman Kodak Company, until his division moved to ITT Industries. Rulon's work at ITT's Space Systems Division involves optimizing image quality of aircraft and satellite imaging. Combining his skill in photography with his passion for birding, he photographs species across North America.

Cover Tom Vezo; 2 Cortez C. Austin Jr.; 12 Cortez C. Austin Jr.; 14 Tom Vezo; 16 Cortez C. Austin Jr.; 18 Cortez C. Austin Jr.; 20 Rulon Simmons; 22 Tom Vezo; 24 Brian E. Small; 26 Tom Vezo; 28 Brian E. Small; 30 Brian E. Small; 32 Brian E. Small; 34 Tom Vezo; 36 Cortez C. Austin Jr.; 38 Tom Vezo; 40 Tom Vezo; 42 Tom Vezo; 44 Tom Brakefield/CORBIS; 46 Brian E. Small; 48 Tom Vezo; 50 Cortez C. Austin Jr.; 52 Cortez C. Austin Jr.; 54 Tom Vezo; 56 Tom Vezo; 58 Tom Vezo; 60 Brian E. Small; 62 Bates Littlehales; 64 Tom Vezo; 66 Tom Vezo; 68 Tom Vezo; 70 Rulon Simmons; 72 Tom Vezo; 74 Tom Vezo; 76 Brian E. Small; 78 Darrell Gulin/CORBIS; 80 Tom Vezo; 82 Bates Littlehales; 84 Tom Vezo; 86 Brian E. Small; 88 Cortez C. Austin Jr.; 90 Tom Vezo; 92 Brian E. Small; 94 Rulon Simmons; 96 Tom Vezo; 98 Tom Vezo; 100 Tom Vezo; 102 Tom Vezo; 104 Cortez C. Austin Jr.; 106 Tom Vezo; 108 Tom Vezo; 110 Brian E. Small; 112 Tom Vezo; 114 Tom Vezo; 116 Tom Vezo; 118 Brian E. Small; 120 Lynda Richardson/CORBIS; 122 Bates Littlehales; 124 Brian E. Small; 126 Tom Vezo; 128 Tom Vezo; 130 Tom Vezo; 132 Bates Littlehales; 134 Tom Vezo; 136 Brian E. Small; 138 Tom Vezo; 140 Tom Vezo; 142 Brian E. Small; 144 Brian E. Small; 146 Tom Vezo; 148 Tom Vezo; 150 Brian E. Small; 152 Tom Vezo; 154 Tom Vezo; 156 Eric and David Hosking/CORBIS; 158 Cortez C. Austin Jr.; 160 Rulon Simmons; 162 Tom Vezo; 164 Brian E. Small; 166 Tom Vezo; 168 Brian E. Small; 170 Brian E. Small; 172 Tom Vezo; 174 Tom Vezo; 176 Tom Vezo; 178 Brian E. Small; 180 Tom Vezo; 182 Bates Littlehales; 184 Brian E. Small; 186 Brian E. Small; 188 Brian E. Small; 190 Cortez C. Austin Jr.; 192 Brian E. Small; 194 Brian E. Small; 196 Tom Vezo; 198 Tom Vezo; 200 Brian E. Small; 202 Bates Littlehales; 204 Ron Austing; Frank Lane Picture Agency/CORBIS; 206 Brian E. Small; 208 Brian E. Small; 210 Tom Vezo; 212 Bates Littlehales; 214 Tom Vezo; 216 Bates Littlehales; 218 Bates Littlehales; 220 Rulon Simmons; 222 Brian E. Small; 224 Brian E. Small; 226 Tom Vezo; 228 Tom Vezo; 230 Tom Vezo; 232 Tom Vezo; 234 Cortez C. Austin Jr.; 236 Brian E. Small; 238 Tom Vezo; 240 Brian E. Small; 242 Tom Vezo; 244 Rulon Simmons; 246 Tom Vezo; 248 Tom Vezo; 250 Rulon Simmons; 252 Brian E. Small; 254 Brian E. Small; 256 Brian E. Small; 258 Tom Vezo

FIELD NOTES

NATIONAL GEOGRAPHIC
FIELD GUIDE TO BIRDS:
MICHIGAN
Edited by Jonathan Alderfer

**Published by
the National Geographic Society**

John M. Fahey, Jr.,
President and Chief Executive Officer

Gilbert M. Grosvenor,
Chairman of the Board

Nina D. Hoffman,
Executive Vice President

Prepared by the Book Division

Kevin Mulroy,
Senior Vice President and Publisher

Kristin Hanneman, *Illustrations Director*

Marianne R. Koszorus, *Design Director*

Carl Mehler, *Director of Maps*

Barbara Brownell Grogan,
Executive Editor

Staff for this Book

Jonathan Alderfer, *Editor*

Dan O'Toole, *Project Manager*

Mary Jo Slazak, *Writer*

Megan McCarthy, *Designer*

Carol Norton, *Series Art Director*

Kristin Hanneman, Dan O'Toole,
Illustrations Editors

Rachel Sweeney, *Illustrations Assistant*

Suzanne Poole, *Text Editor*

Matt Chwastyk,
Map Production

Rick Wain, *Production Project Manager*

Manufacturing and Quality Control

Christopher A. Liedel,
Chief Financial Officer

Phillip L. Schlosser, *Managing Director*

John T. Dunn, *Technical Director*

One of the world's largest nonprofit scientific and educational organizations, the National Geographic Society was founded in 1888 "for the increase and diffusion of geographic knowledge." Fulfilling this mission, the Society educates and inspires millions every day through its magazines, books, television programs, videos, maps and atlases, research grants, the National Geographic Bee, teacher workshops, and innovative classroom materials. The Society is supported through membership dues, charitable gifts, and income from the sale of its educational products. This support is vital to National Geographic's mission to increase global understanding and promote conservation of our planet through exploration, research, and education.

For more information, please call
1-800-NGS LINE (647-5463) or write
to the following address:

National Geographic Society
1145 17th Street N.W.
Washington, D.C. 20036-4688 U.S.A.

Visit the Society's Web site at
www.nationalgeographic.com.

**Library of Congress
Cataloging-in-Publication Data**
Available upon request.